PASSING IT ON

SHORT TALKS ON TRIBAL FIGHTING ON THE NORTH-WEST FRONTIER OF INDIA

By

GENERAL SIR ANDREW SKEEN
K.C.B., K.C.I.E., C.M.G.

With a Foreword by
HIS EXCELLENCY GENERAL SIR PHILIP W. CHETWODE
G.C.B., K.C.M.G., D.S.O.
Commander-in-Chief in India.

The Naval & Military Press Ltd

PREFACE

WHEN young, I once had cause to thank a senior for his wise teaching of the needs of frontier fighting. His reply was: "That's all right, youngster, pass it on." I acted on it during the rest of my service, and am doing it now, in the only way left to me.

* * * *

This book is addressed to the junior officer of Infantry, of the British Service in particular, as he is less likely in his wider range of service to be trained for the local problem which all officers in India have to keep in mind. To officers of Infantry, because that is the arm on which falls in chief part the need for adjusting its methods to the circumstances of this special form of war. And to junior officers, because in frontier fighting the junior officer's problems are many and varied, and their correct solution far more important in immediate results than in any other form of war.

* * * *

My readers must forgive the personal approach. I find it easier to write as I used to speak when I taught. It also, I think, avoids too close a likeness to the Training Manuals, which can sometimes be indigestible to the young soldier.

CONTENTS

CHAPTER I

GENERAL ... ...   PAGE 1

Tribal country, its character; and that of its men—Their fighting qualities—Analysed, we find they can be neutralized by fire and movement, by alertness, and by cunning.

CHAPTER II

STILL GENERAL 12

Changes in tribal methods—Other factors adding to our difficulties due to the High Velocity Rifle—Increasing slowness of movement in the hills due mainly to the same thing—The Permanent Piquet a product of the same thing, which will also enforce advance in touch with motorable roadhead.

CHAPTER III

INTRODUCING DETAIL 23

The "Manual" must be the guide—Bird's-eye view of a Column on the march, in its various activities.

CHAPTER IV

ASPECTS OF WORK FALLING TO JUNIOR OFFICERS ON THE MARCH 31

Work with the Vanguard; and with the Transport.

CHAPTER V

ASPECTS OF WORK FALLING TO JUNIOR OFFICERS ON THE MARCH—*Continued* 41

Junior Officers' work with the flank piquets.

CHAPTER VI

ASPECTS OF WORK FALLING TO JUNIOR OFFICERS ON THE MARCH—*Concluded* 53

Junior Officers' work with the flank piquets, and with the rear guard.

CHAPTER VII

ASPECTS OF WORK FALLING TO JUNIOR OFFICERS IN TAKING UP CAMP 62

Occupation of protective piquet positions by the advanced guard—Work of camp colour parties—Principles of layout and protection of a perimeter camp—Occupation of camp piquets.

CHAPTER VIII

ASPECTS OF WORK FALLING TO JUNIOR OFFICERS IN TAKING UP CAMP—*Continued* 77

Occupation of perimeter defences and subsequent work—Occupation of a village in emergency—Points to be guarded against in camp—Sniping—Assault—Daily Routine.

CHAPTER IX

ASPECTS OF WORK FALLING TO JUNIOR OFFICERS PUTTING UP PERMANENT PIQUETS 86

Slow process of putting up permanent piquets—The operation—Dispositions to cover the work—The work—Duties after occupation and in succeeding days—The value of the system—Convoy escort duty—Dangers of the " Raghza "—The floating platoon.

CHAPTER X

ASPECTS OF WORK FALLING TO JUNIOR OFFICERS WHEN A COLUMN MOVES 101

Early preparations and start of advanced guard—Preliminary work of rear guard—Duties with transport—Rear guard activities.

CHAPTER XI

ASPECTS OF WORK FALLING TO JUNIOR OFFICERS IN ATTACK AND WITHDRAWAL 107

Opportunity for a " formal " attack seldom offers ; and must be taken fully when given—Distribution ; and points to guard against—Further action in case of an advance —Or of a withdrawal—Ravines and other dangers—Danger of intersected and bushy country—Night work.

CHAPTER XII

ASPECTS OF WORK FALLING TO JUNIOR OFFICERS IN FORAGING AND DEMOLITION 119

Foraging equipment—Organization for the work—Points to be watched, and methods found safest and best—Constant vigilance needed—Method of withdrawal—Demolition, a more serious matter—Organization for the work, and methods of destruction—Manner of withdrawal.

FOREWORD

BY

HIS EXCELLENCY GENERAL SIR PHILIP W. CHETWODE,
G.C.B., K.C.M.G., D.S.O.,
Commander-in-Chief in India.

THERE are few soldiers with a wider knowledge of Indian Frontier Warfare than General Sir Andrew Skeen, and it is greatly to our advantage that he has put some of this knowledge at our disposal.

His chapters do not aim at replacing the official regulations, but supplement them with a wealth of first-hand experience.

This book will be of great value to all who need to study Indian Frontier Warfare, and more particularly to those who lack the advantage of familiarity with the local atmosphere and conditions.

P. C.

June, 1932.

CHAPTER I.

GENERAL.

Tribal country, its character; and that of its men—Their fighting qualities—Analysed, we find they can be neutralized by fire and movement, by alertness, and by cunning.

"WHAT is the North-West Frontier like? The country and its fighting men?" This, in one form or another, is a question often shot at me, even now. Not easy to answer. In fact, it cannot be answered in a few words. Though I have footslogged or ridden most of the frontier from Mastuj to Kalat, I can only tell you that no short stretch of it is like its neighbour, and that a description of it as a whole is bound to mislead. You will never find ground of the same nature for twenty miles on end. First, miles of cliff and stony slopes giving way to open fans of cultivation backed by steeps and sheer cliffs, narrow river gorges opening out of fir-covered mountains, which drop to swelling bush-covered hills or bare grazing grounds with patches of forest. Then open plains flanked by low, bare hills, and scored by deep ravines, after which you come to the great bare hills and cliffs of the Khaibar, and so on through wooded Maidan and Mastura and Khanki, and the bare Kurram and Tochi valleys to the hills of Mahsud Waziristan, ilex covered in the centre, deodar forest on the mountains which dominate the strips of open downs, scrub and shale-covered hills in the lower parts, and, most dangerous of all, the bush-tufted, stony plains and ravines where the dashing tactics of the Mahsud find their fullest scope. And then the opener country of the Gomal and the Zhob, until near Peshin the tribal country is left for the kindlier open stretches of Quetta and Kalat, and there my knowledge ends.

But in no one place are conditions a guide to what may be found in another, and only principles can help you to use your men to the best advantage in any part; while for details you will be wiser if you turn to the military reports of the particular areas you are to work in than to trust to the memory of one who has not been in any of them for some years.

* * * *

The people differ less than do the parts they live in. All are men to reckon with. I place the Mahsud highest as a fighter along with the Mamund, a little folk but stark. The Afridi probably comes third—his blood feuds and sectional quarrels make him a little less ready to die. But all are apt in war, and taken all in all are probably the finest individual fighters in the east, really formidable enemies, to despise whom means sure trouble.

They have a great reputation for cunning, which really is based on great mobility on cliffs and steep slopes, marked ability, which their warring life fosters, to make use of ground to hide their movements and to protect them when not moving, great patience, and intimate knowledge of the ground.

Mobility is a weak word for the tribesman's power of movement. In pursuit, where everything holds out promise of success, these fellows are wonderful. They come down hillsides like falling boulders, not running but bounding, and in crags they literally drop from foothold to foothold. To deal with such mobility on their own lines is impossible. These men are hard as nails; they live on little, carry nothing but a rifle and a few cartridges, a knife and a bit of food, and they are shod for quick and sure movement. Against all this you can only ensure that your men are hard, and can move quickly and surely on broken ground and stony slopes. Add that the tribesman can always move behind a screen of hills and ravines or under cover of night, and in mobility the balance is well against you. But you can redress it by the things in which you and your men should excel—discipline and fire power. Use these to combine fire and movement, whether that movement be forward or backward, and handicaps of heavy boots and equipment and the enemy's freedom to select the point of attack fall into their proper place. Indeed, this very mobility of theirs may often lead them too far and give you a better chance of killing, which is the only way to make the tribesman feel defeat.

Their power of moving concealed is astounding, not only in moving from cover to cover, but in slipping from light to shadow, and background to background. It has to be seen to be believed. And their stillness in cover is equally striking. You can never train your men to the same pitch, but you can do a great deal. And another way in which you can train your men, one which is seldom tried, is in using their eyes. Next time you have your men out on field training, watch them. I wager you will find all of them except, I hope, yourself, engrossed in anything but what should be engrossing them—that is, the possible enemy. Thomas Atkins thinks of the future, or of special incidents of the past, his eyes on the ground or on a comrade, or on a cigarette, while Sundar Singh, his Indian opposite number, is intent on what is to be done when the expectant buffalo at home has calved, or on some such homely interest; but not one is really concentrating on the job in hand unless specially ordered to.

I have a memory of part of a famous frontier battalion held up on a ridge by snipers on the flank whom they could not locate, and of two guns coming up to help, spotting the snipers in less than twenty seconds, and dispersing them with a couple of rounds. This particular battery had a system of training which produced super look-outs, human wolves, red-eyed with watching for victims, but what they did, any troops can do. So when you go to India, take your first leave shooting in Chamba or Kulu, or some wild part of Kashmir, and learn to use eyes and glasses in the hills. And then use your knowledge to train your men in keeping their eyes moving whether halted or on the move. With many young eyes quartering the front and watching every ridge and rock and bush, no enemy movement should escape you, and you will be ready for them.

And that brings me to the tribesman's patience. These folk have nothing to do but to watch for an opportunity. If it doesn't come one day, it is bound to come the next or the next, or, at any rate often enough to make it worth their while to watch for it. And if, when it comes, it looks like being too costly, they are perfectly ready to put it off till a better chance comes. Remember, they have no work to do, no camp to get to, they have range upon range of hill to screen them for as long as they choose, and night has no terrors for them. They will return to the job day after day without anyone having an inkling of their presence, and then when the real chance comes they seize it like lightning.

* * * *

Now, at the risk of boring you, here is the sort of thing that happens.

In 1919, a piquet of some 60 men held a hill overlooking the Tochi River at some distance and securing a big stretch of road near Miranshah. Each morning this piquet had to send out a day party of ten rifles to hold a knoll about eighty yards off which overlooked a side ravine. Between the knoll and the main piquet lay a bit of dead ground, and so each morning the entire piquet stood to arms in its " sangar " to cover the passage of the detached party to its day post. Days passed, quiet and deadly dull, and standing to at dawn became a tiresome duty, and then a neglected one. Where thirty or more rifles had watched the knoll, a sleepy sentry now followed the party moving out with lack-lustre eyes. Then, one morning, as the day party reached the dead ground, a blast of fire downed it, while another swept the " sangar " and for ten minutes kept its occupants firing blindly and intermittently, while a bunch of the enemy dashed into the dead ground, secured the rifles and most of the ammunition of the day party, and legged it. Fire slackened, and then ceased, and the occupants of the piquet issued to find the enemy several hundreds yards off, and ten of their comrades dead.

So far, you see, only bad work on the part of the piquet, and an opportunity seized by the enemy. Yes—but let us see it from the enemy's side. Five days before the raid, a party of about forty Mahsuds had arrived at some caves nine miles south of the piquet across the Tochi. They must have had previous knowledge of the ground and some idea of the habits of the piquet, for the very first night they occupied the knoll and got ready. Then, about midnight, a star fell from an unlucky direction, and this omen caused a silent retreat. Next night the Tochi was swollen and they could not cross. The next night they had nearly reached the hill when the dogs in a village they had passed began to howl. This might have startled the piquet, thought the raiders, so back they tramped the weary miles to their lair. The next night all went well, and they got into position. The night wore on and one unwary lad stood up and relieved himself. The elders of the party at once concluded that the sound must have been carried by the wind to the piquet, and once more the trail to the caves was taken. On the fifth night all went well, and as each man carried a stem of dwarf palm down which to direct the flow, they avoided the noise of many waters. At dawn their reward came, the day party issued, entered the fringe of the dead ground, and were immediately shot down by part of the gang, the rest of whom kept the piquet under subjection as described. It that doesn't show patience, I don't know what does, and I take off my hat to that bunch of raiders. They deserved what they won.

* * * *

You will now want to know how you are to deal with this " patience " danger. The solution—never relax any precautions—is obvious and easy to state, but devilish hard to apply because it is not natural to keep nerves and imagination on the stretch when there is apparently nothing to justify it. That is the trouble—day after day, whether on baggage escort or convoy or covering duties or patrol or any of the duties on which a young officer may be off on his own, you will see nothing but bare hills or rock or bush, quiet as the grave, and on your part nothing but a weary track or hillside to be trod.

It needs a great effort of will to keep yourself and your men alert, but if you are not, however empty the hillsides may be one minute, you may be paying the penalty the next. For remember the enemy is always there, and looking for you to make a mistake. I don't say every mistake brings its punishment, but I do say that though you may make one mistake and if your luck is in two or three, all the time you are marked by unseen eyes as likely to give chances, and it will not be long before you know it. Conversely, if you are spotted as alert, and your battalion as one not to be monkeyed with, its reputation will spread behind the hills, and the raider will look for easier prey.

* * * *

Here is another instance of the repeated mistake and its punishment.

To give freedom in patrolling on one of the guarded sections of the Tochi road, to avoid the risk to weak patrols issuing from piquets, and to give those patrols a chance of effecting surprise and of varying their route each day, a system was started called "The Floating Platoon." A quaint name, but the most descriptive to be found. A lightly equipped platoon moved up and down as the spirit moved it on the flanks of the road between the permanent piquets, and at nightfall billeted itself on any suitable piquet, resuming its work at dawn and moving back to a main camp at reasonable intervals for rest. The guiding principle was that on no two successive nights was the platoon to be at the same piquet. The system was most successful till this principle was abused, and one of the platoons for some reason spent three nights in one piquet. In fact, the floating platoon ceased floating, and of course this was spotted by the enemy.

The first night, naturally, nothing happened, but when the platoon returned to the piquet for the second night the watchers seemed to have pricked their ears to some purpose, for on the fourth morning when the platoon left and came down the apparently safeguarded slopes in full view of the piquets across the valley, moving on two adjacent spurs and all according to Cocker, it was completely wiped out by two parties of tribesmen in ground dead to the piquet just issued from, each enfilading the troops coming down the spur to their right or left.

So far, only good tactics, but each party of the enemy had taken steps to protect itself from being seen from the piquets across the valley by building thin stone walls at their backs, and were crouching in the open to meet the men coming down from the piquet. One night to stop the possibility of a scoop and the next night to lay the trap with every precaution against its being detected.

One can't help admiring these folk, and if we don't take lessons from their doings, we deserve all we get.

* * * *

They are equally careful with their minor ambushes, and clever as can be with them. This is not surprising, for they have constant practice in their daily life in conditions where a mistake means death. They have full knowledge of the ground which they have grazed their goats over since childhood, protective colouring to a marked degree in their filthy rags, good eyesight, and instinct for danger, without which they could not survive in this land of blood feud and inter-tribal war. Take one example only, the Khuzma Nullah incident. Here a party moving in a little valley were fired on from the left. No one was visible, but the party did the right thing and dashed with fixed bayonets up the slope towards the shot. And as soon as they were spread-eagled thus, a blast of fire from the right dropped the lot. Probably no sign of anything till the burst of fire, and then the swift rush with knives, the stripping of the dead, and the unhurried mutilation of the infidels. Yet a portion of the party a short way behind whence they could cover with fire might at least have saved the ambush from becoming a slaughter place. You see how the commander of the smallest parties has always to be thinking, for he is out against men who know their own game well, and play it hard.

* * * *

But there is no need to become discouraged with tales of fiendish cunning and unescapable disaster. Fire and movement should be your slogan, and why should you not on your side use cunning? I see no reason why an active minded man who can put himself into the enemy's skin should not outwit him quite often enough to put the fear of death into him. And once that is done be sure that the battalion which does it well will get a name for it, and in all its little independent or detached duties will be given a wide berth, just as surely as the one which is known to be heavy and dull is selected as a victim.

How are you to do it? Think out evil little dodges. The best known is the " Silly Fool " piquet. On a suitable occasion the men of a piquet get up slackly, dust their seats, pick up rifles by the muzzle, and slope off under loud words of command a few steps down hill, leaving bright lookouts in cover. The enemy, if there, make a rush for the discarded piquet position, and is met by the full strength of the piquet at short range. I have seen this worked twice. The second time was certainly against Afghan Mohmands, not quite the wily folk our tribesmen are, but it worked admirably. The officer who ran it was a first-class lad, and his men were Gurkhas; but you are a first-class lad, and there is no reason why your men should not lie low as well as Gurkhas.

That is only one way. Lying-out for snipers after dark is another. Note the "lying-out," for nothing will be done if you patrol. Movement spoils all. Therefore, if you are going to set a proper night " chapao " or ambush, settle into it and conceal yourselves as early in the afternoon as you would if sitting up for a tiger, for you don't know where the human tiger may be watching from. And distract him, as you do the tiger, by having men moving naturally about and clearing off normally, and then leaving you and your men to the night and luck. Or else move out to the place, if near, after dark, settle in and lie low. But there must be no silly idea of stalking at night. The man who moves gives himself away, and to do any good himself the enemy must approach, and in doing so may be got. By the way, when you go in for night work, in the absence of a brigade sign, you should have a recognition signal. Light taps on the pouch or on the pocket if pouches are discarded, are good and can be varied. The butt of the rifle is not so good as the enemy have butts to play tunes on also. But have a signal—it may prevent much palpitation and possible accidents.

But there are other ways, without risk, all of the booby trap type. A guncotton charge in a dud grave will discourage desecration of graves, a nice little habit of these folk, and is far better than the old dodge of burying a mule or litter above the body. A similar charge, complete with friction tube, will do in a sportsman cutting cable. This is a very common annoyance, not done for military reasons but to secure a really stout material for stringing the family bed; and if as our friend runs merrily along coiling up quarter of a mile of usefulness he finds the cable checked, he will naturally think it is a bush or stone, give the cable a jerk, and himself be jerked noisily across Jordan. That usually chokes off all cable cutting for a bit. Another, best ordered by higher authority, is an ammunition box with guncotton for contents, and a friction tube on the split pin, realistically dropped in withdrawal; a stout group will certainly gather round this best of all loot to share it out, *et voila!* Cad trick, but all booby traps are more or less that, and when you fight with dogs you must bite like a wolf.

* * * *

But you have only to sit down and think out ways. You can easily outwit the Pathan if you set out to do it, because by setting traps instead of walking into them you take the initiative and keep him guessing. Moreover, he is used to our blundering, straightforward ways of war, and a change to his own ways upsets him badly. I have tried this and know it. When we forced the Barari Tangi we had a lot of men out against us, and few enough to tackle them with. So we first took some heights to the south, and put a stout piquet on it. This was necessary in any case. Then we put up a similarly necessary one north of the Tangi. There was an important height in the centre, just above the Tangi, and a piquet had to be put on that. So we gambled on the enemy thinking the next move would just mean the same old piquet building which they could harass as usual about 11 a.m., and no point in getting up earlier. It worked, and as a result, we got through the Tangi and occupied a really appalling ridge beyond with something under twenty casualties, a job which would have cost us at least a hundred if the enemy had been ready for us. Mystify and mislead—the old rule. Nothing new in it, but how often forgotten!

Another time, which I shall never forget as it was the worst night of mental misery I have gone through, was the withdrawal of two distant camp piquets at Makin. We wanted to get the bulk of our camp off quietly, but of course the enemy knew we were clearing some day and were ready to worry us. Had the two piquets been brought in as they ought to have been, decently and in order during the day, the gaff would have been blown and we would have had snipers round us all night and packs of them at dawn. All right when you haven't some fifteen hundred transport animals to load and pass out, bad when you have. So the piquets were ordered to come away half an hour after the moon set, about 2.30 a.m. Why after the moon set? Put yourself in the Pathans' skin. They knew we were unlikely to move in the dark in preference to moonlight, and, so, though they were all round the piquets at 2 a.m., they went off to a well-earned sleep shortly after, and both piquets came through without casualty. And next morning the enemy woke to find the camp gone, and the fighting portion of the column ready for them. A great deal was due to the officers and men of the piquets—a most gallant feat, but if they had not waited it would have been the last time they ever left a piquet.

The truth is, you can do a great deal that seems risky, provided you put yourself in the enemy's place, think as he would, and then don't do what he expects you to. And when he has been fooled two or three times, play for a change the straight silly game he is accustomed to from us, and his heart will break.

This applies to every act, from the decisions of the higher commanders to the handling of the section by the latest lance-corporal. One of the reasons why the Pathan has been so successful in the past and has such a reputation for cunning is that he has reckoned on our playing the obvious soldier's game, and has been right. Copy his game, and go one better, and he is done.

CHAPTER II.

STILL GENERAL.

Changes in tribal methods—Other factors adding to our difficulties due to the High Velocity Rifle—Increasing slowness of movement in the hills due mainly to the same thing—The Permanent Piquet a product of the same thing, which will also enforce advance in touch with motorable roadhead.

THE greatest change so far in tribal methods and in the steps needed to counter them has been brought about by the high velocity rifle and by smokeless powder. The first has, of course, added to the tribesman's power for harm, but it has done more than that. It has made every valley into a " Tangi," or defile, and in place of piquets covering the close vicinity of columns on the move or in camp, we now have to hold heights at any distance up to fifteen hundred yards and more from it. Longer to reach, more loss in taking them, more men to hold them, and harder to get away from—the whole meaning slower movement of the force they are posted to protect. When I started this game, seizing a piquet position was a simple thing, taking the time it took to scale some point overlooking the line of march at three hundred yards or so, and when you got to it you hadn't to expect bullets snickering in from far off and from somewhere you couldn't see. And holding it was equally simple, for though sometimes overlooked at the then effective range, it was not practically always overlooked as at present. So that direct casualties were few and attack uphill at close quarters covered by an accurate long range fire was not known.

As for smokeless powder—in the old days you knew at once where the enemy were, by large and frequent puffs of smoke from anything up to elephant rifles, and to hit you, they had to be close enough to be seen quite easily. In the fighting against the Mahsuds in 1919 and

1920, I was at my command post during twenty-three actions in which at least a brigade was employed, with anything from three hundred to five thousand men up against us. From the nature of things the command post was inside a semi-circle of fighting men, so I saw everything, and during the whole of that time I only saw two puffs of black powder.

This power of remaining unseen in action, increased of course by the longer ranges at which hurt can be inflicted, has led to more care in keeping out of sight. At the Malakand in '97, the hillsides were like a field of flowers with the standards erected by the enemy. We used to reckon one standard as supported by fifty men. Not quite so many at the Malakand, where the looting of the bazaar had made standards about two a penny. Now, flags are seldom seen, and the " void of the battlefield " is as marked as anywhere else.

* * * *

There is one difference, however. In modern war the problem is to get over beaten zones, and safe passage is for the individual a matter of luck. In frontier fighting, you will soon know the difference. No shots are fired except at a mark, and in place of the impersonal killing of the Great War you will find that you yourself have been picked to be shot at by a most persistent enemy, and pretty closely missed, if at all. Quite unpleasant, and difficult to get used to, especially as you never know nowadays where the marksman is.

* * * *

It is curious how the odds change. At the Umbeyla Pass, in the sixties, where the tribes from North of the Kabul River combined to hold up a fair-sized force for several weeks, the enemy's weapon, the jezail, with a range of three hundred yards or so, completely out-matched the Brown Bess of our troops. And the fighting developed into a series of bitter struggles for piquet positions, and ceased with the exhaustion of the enemy.

Then the Brown Bess was replaced by the Snider, and we were on top. Following on came the Martini Henry, twice the fellow the Snider was. Then came the Lee Metford and smokeless powder, used by the British battalions in 1897 for the first time, and startling the Bunerwals at the Tanga Pass out of their lives. All this time the tribesmen had been wallowing along with their jezails and odd guns and a sprinkling of stolen Sniders and later Martinis, so that as late as 1915 frontier fighting remained for us a pleasant enough way of applying peace training with enough of danger in it to make it exciting, unpleasantly so when the principles of war and the special methods demanded by tribal tactics were ignored.

Modern arms had been slowly arriving through the Gulf and Afghanistan, though so costly that they were few; but with the war there was an increase in the flow, from Mesopotamia and elsewhere, and finally the defection of parts of the Waziristan Militias armed the Mahsud really well.

In the 1919 affair, so fully were the Mahsuds alive to the value of their improved armament that no black powder weapons were allowed into the fight by day, and their application of fire was carefully organized. Long range sniping, and covering fire from all ranges to let the swordsmen close. And the lack of musketry training in all but a few units and the marksmanship of the Mahsud gave back to the tribesmen the superiority which they had lost with the arrival of the Snider. Then the wheel came full circle, and in the fighting for the piquets at Palosina, in Christmas week of 1919, the Umbeyla was reproduced, in its staggering beginning, its anxious battling, and its end—in the Mahsud losses on Black Hill, which sent them back to lick their wounds till we advanced again.

But now our powerful pack guns, our machine guns, our small arms training, and our ample ammunition supply should have wiped out this advantage, and all that remains is to bring your men up to a standard in this form of fighting which will counterbalance the many natural advantages which the tribesmen possess.

* * * *

In another way our troubles have increased of late, and that is in increased unhandiness of forces operating in these hills. In 1860 a move from Jandola to Makin took four days. In 1920 it took two months. The reasons are many. One, unavoidable, is the increased fighting power of the enemy, requiring something stronger than the columns of three or four battalions or less which have frequently in the past traversed tribal country and smashed opposition. The same factor demands the carriage of vastly increased reserves of ammunition, of explosives, of wire, Very lights, tools, sandbags, and the thousand and one aids which we never dreamed of asking for of old. Then, with the increased grip of the doctors on our medical arrangements, ambulance strengths have increased. Excellent, of course, and public opinion will never allow less, but none the less hampering, and if public opinion demands satisfaction in this direction it must be prepared for slower work. And, lastly, the weight of ration carried has doubled for the troops, and the wretched non-combatants are at last decently fed and clothed. And as it has become impossible to protect grazing animals, the camel now has to have some food carried for him. The results more than justify it. Sick lists are smaller, work is more efficient, and all that; but it all means more transport in proportion to the fighting man, and therefore slower work. In short, increased enemy fighting power and increased impedimenta combine so to slow down movement that I hold the only economical way of dealing with a powerful tribal resistance to be by an advance a short distance ahead of motorable roadhead. Any other method means vast expense eventually, and many possibilities of disaster all the time.

That brings me to another innovation—the Permanent Piquet. Until the high velocity rifle imposed the various conditions of delay which I have mentioned, columns could be smaller and were less unwieldy, and the system of flanking piquets sent out from a force on the move and withdrawn with its rearguard was found to be the best form of protection on the march. But it has now been shown that if there is likely to be serious opposition, ordinary piquet posting becomes a long matter and a march of any length, in consequence, an impossibility. A system more economical of time and of life had to be devised to meet the changed circumstances which we met in the Mahsud campaign.

The Manual * says: " Permanent Piquets are more economical and secure," but there are many more and stronger reasons for their employment when tackling a well-armed enemy. In the old days putting up a flanking piquet was a simple matter, short distances to go and come back from, and remarkably little opposition, generally only sniping from not too accurate weapons. In fact, I have only seen three such piquets strongly opposed out of the hundreds I must have seen put up. Assault, if it developed later in the day, was a scrap between men with swords and pistols without covering fire to help them, and troops armed with rifle and bayonet, in possession of higher ground. So that the force, whether a fighting column or a convoy, was little delayed by the process of flank protection. Now, piquets have to go long distances, are far more liable to losses when in position, usually require support to their withdrawal, and have a bad time generally. And the time taken in posting and withdrawal is immensely increased.

Further, if this sort of thing has to be undertaken by forces escorting transport, apart from the slower movement, they have to be strong out of all proportion to

---

* *Manual of Operations on the North-West Frontier of India.* Army Headquarters, India, 1925.

the columns in front and even then risk loss and possible disaster every day. So I think that wherever a well-armed and tenacious enemy has to be tackled you will find that except for foraging expeditions or movement of lightly equipped columns ahead of the advanced base—in fact, wherever an advance is being made along what is intended to be the main line of communications—a system of permanent piquets will be adopted.

This must mean that the campaign takes the form of a series of short marches, each followed by halts, during which supplies are filled up, sick evacuated, and permanent piquets established behind and in front of the halting place, to secure the communications behind and ensure a flying start for the next move. This process will naturally be a lengthy one. In 1919-1920 in Waziristan, though several factors made the initial moves slow, at the end you still had a very efficient force taking over a day per mile to advance up a wide riverbed leaving a securely held passage behind it. On this basis it should not be impossible to drive a road traversable by at least six-wheeler motor transport behind the troops with no more delay than will inevitably occur without it; while the fact that troops will be employed rather in covering road construction than in forcing an ill-supported entry into undeveloped country will allow of three very desirable things. Economy of troops, always to be sought after; economy of camel transport which is necessary if we are not to exhaust a by no means too rich source of essential animals; and lastly, an enemy compelled by shame to attack on ground of our own choosing rather than as in the past on ground of his own choosing whenever it suited him to use it.

So if circumstances demand an advance covered by construction and occupation of permanent piquets, they should also justify the construction of motorable roads immediately behind it, instead of later, after time, money, men, and transport have been used up in an attempt to apply the old style of operation to present conditions.

In these remarks I have had in mind only an invasion of enemy country, contested bitterly as such invasion will usually be until the enemy sees the futility of resistance. Such invasions will, I trust, disappear in time if the policy which has been so successful in Waziristan is applied to other parts of the frontier. That is to say—if tribal areas, once penetrated on due occasion, are permanently occupied and opened out by driving roads through them. Instead of, as in the past, years of humiliating outrage forcing on us a bloody campaign, ending in more or less harried withdrawal, let us have occupation and roads. Roads, which, apart from their civilizing effects, give lightly equipped columns the power to concentrate and operate within a circuit of several days action off good communications. Then the whole weary business of communications and unwieldy columns disappears, and the problem of military control of the area is simplified as far as such a problem can ever be.

* * * *

Other changes are all in our favour. Guns have become immensely more powerful. In my early days the only gun was the 7-pdr. " bubble and squeak " gun, a most useful weapon in support, but, of course, with nothing like the power or range of the 10-pdr. which followed it. Quick into action, and throwing a shell sufficiently heavy for ordinary work, this still was unable to cause real losses by frontal fire. Then came the 2.75-inch gun, more powerful and with a longer range, but still without much killing power against men behind cover. Last came the 3.7-inch howitzer, accurate and death-dealing with either shrapnel or high explosive shell, and with ample range, and with only two "crabs" as far as I know—the weight of shell to be carried and the weight of some of the gun loads. The one adds to the ammunition columns, and the other lowers the gun's mobility. The pack guns can no longer be expected to " climb up the side of a sign board and trust to the stick of the paint," but as their power of indirect fire makes this no longer necessary, it doesn't matter. In this respect then, we have an immense advantage, speedily recognized by the Mahsuds, who sent in to complain that the new gun wasn't fair; and from their fine old-world standpoint it wasn't. It never gave them a chance.

So we have the pull in our guns, and you have only to see a rush of tribesmen over a crest in pursuit, and the pack guns at work on them, to see what a need there is for guns; and, incidentally, for practice in co-operation between infantry and pack artillery whenever possible.

The value of machine guns in this sort of fighting is obvious. Gun support cannot be done without, but gun ammunition is heavy to carry and hard to replace in action, so the infantry cannot expect a constant artillery support, but a section of machine guns, well handled, should make it impossible for an enemy to hold a ridge against the close approach of infantry or to press pursuit beyond the crests or flanks of hills. Handy, accurate, and mobile—the machine gun should be all the Manual claims for it.

Then the Very light. A small thing, but the difference it can make. Formerly, we had only the star shell, to use which meant rousing the whole camp and using up a very valuable thing, or the flares we used to place carefully to our front, which once used up could not be replaced till daylight, and which often did not work. Now, every small portion of the force, piquet or camp, can illuminate danger, and the knowledge is very soothing to the nerves. On the other hand, like all good things, it can be abused, and later I shall impress this on you. But it is one of the new things which have arrived to help us to the detriment of Brother Pathan.

Then the hand grenade. This relic of the past, which came again into most effective being in the Great War, has added a lot to our advantages. For searching out dead ground, for dealing with attackers closing on to a piquet, and for dislodging men in thick cover it and its cousin the rifle grenade are hard to beat. And in clearing out huts and caves it is a life-saver, or rather a casualty avoider, without equal. A hole in the roof and a bomb lobbed in, and all the danger attending a dash into gloom out of daylight is gone. Sundry inventors, recognizing this, had already produced hairbrush and other guncotton devilments for the same purpose, but never anything approaching the Mills grenade for this particular task.

The trench mortar has its uses, but I think the pack howitzer fills the bill better in any work the trench mortar can do, while supreme for its own job as well. Still, the rate of fire of a Stokes Mortar, its shattering noise, its lightness and cheapness, are all to the good, and in it we might find another aid for the regular soldier.

I have never seen smoke in action, but have studied it in service surroundings. It also has its dangers, but its uses should far outweigh these. Remember that the enemy has not much in the way of ammunition, and what he has he likes to use against something he can see roll over. So he will not loose off unless he can draw a bead, and this being so a flank screen of smoke if the wind suits will help in advance or withdrawal. I should think twice before laying it down on a crest about to be left—it gives too good a screen for pursuers to move behind; unless, of course, it were possible to use a whiff of gas occasionally with the smoke to inspire caution in the pursuit.

Then armoured vehicles. When I left there were serious objections to using the track type, chief being the impossibility of maintaining them in the field beyond touch with railhead. But armoured cars were in frequent use, and their speed, volume of fire, and security for the crews made them a formidable asset in ground where they could be used. And this was far more frequent than one would think, particularly among the foothills and the tricky ground found there. I should hate to be without them anywhere where they could be used.

And lastly, the air. My only experience of air action was in 1919-1920. There even the out-of-date planes used were invaluable, especially during the bad days. Handled by as gallant a lot of lads as could be wished for, they were constantly in the fight, giving help in attack and withdrawal which no ground arm could have done. Their actual effect was not great, but the moral effect was enormous, for they kept the enemy crouching while near him, and as they appeared, the tails of the soldiery went up, and when they went off to refill, tails went down. So much so that in view of the raw and somewhat rattled state of the infantry, I had to strive to have one of my few planes in the air all the time. Nowadays their value must be far greater.

You may say that one of the main difficulties of mountain operations should have disappeared, and that the blind column groping along a valley is a thing of the past. I doubt it. In 1919 at least, information was too deceptive to be useful, and practice did not improve matters. I remember so well after three months' work and practice getting a report from the advanced aerodrome that the two planes up with us at the heaviest day's fighting at Makin had reported no sign of the enemy. I sympathized fully with their despair, good lads that they were, when ninety casualties were reported for that day. It was no fault of theirs—we had repeatedly to exhort them not to fly so low, for they were taking risks all the time in their efforts to help. But no one could have spotted those ragged grey-clothed fighters crouched among rock and grey ilex. From the ground it was hard, from the air it must have been impossible.

I will not enter into the bitter controversy which always arises as to the power of the Air Force to deal with tribal areas on its own. My own view is that these people are really so invulnerable in their miserable property, and in their persons save from accurate and close range use of ground weapons, and are moreover so scattered and so adept at cover and concealment that I doubt whether any tribe that has the will to resist will ever be coerced by air action alone. I think the Haji of Turangzai and his Mohmand friends agree with me.

CHAPTER III.

INTRODUCING DETAIL.

The "Manual" must be the guide—Bird's-eye view of a Column on the march, in its various activities.

So far I have avoided detail, and you may be feeling that a junior officer would be better given something of practical use—hints how to handle his platoon or company and so forth. I am going to do so, but this is delicate ground. It is quite likely that if you and your company started to train on the lines I think sound, your commanding officer might drop on you, for when all is said and done he is responsible for the training in his battalion. And even if he approved he might well be up against his brigadier. Also, when you go to India, you will find stress laid on frontier fighting, and all battalions in your brigade will no doubt be trained by your brigadier on lines approved if not laid down by his Divisional Commander, and based on the "Manual of Operations on the North-West Frontier of India," a book which I advise you to study. Again, though I hope I was well up-to-date when I left India, recent scrapping may have brought fresh lessons, and my knowledge, once very full, may now be less useful. But this isn't very likely—I and my generation trained on lines following closely in principle those taught by Lumsden of the Guides, and others who died many years before you were born, and except for changes in method due to smokeless ammunition and the high velocity rifle, we found the teaching good. So I will give you my experience, trusting you to make yourself fully acquainted with the principles and practice set down in the Manual. Stick to them and only use what I am to tell you to amplify where necessary the rather compressed information in that book.

One complaint I have heard against the book is that, full and clear though it is, it cannot from the nature of it show to the novice what the various operations look like. So what I propose to do now is to tell you what I have been accustomed to see, to give you, as far as I can, a sort of bird's-eye view of a phase of operations and then deal with the detail of the work which may fall to the junior officer in his part of the whole. And as the most important, in its frequency and its chances of danger, is a march in the mountains, I have chosen that.

Here the Manual certainly does not give a clear picture, though it deals faithfully with the main activities. Nor does peace training even in India show it fully, because it is difficult in peace to reproduce fully what is there in operations. Let me try.

Suppose yourself to be watching from aloft the slow movement of a column in the mountains. It may be moving along a wide, dry river bed, and its length may be, say, some four miles in such a case; or it may be trailing along a narrow mule path, in which case it may cover twelve miles or more. But what you will see first in any case is a couple or more lines of men leapfrogging and carefully covering each other in the process, but stretching only a short distance on each side of the track. These are infantry of the advanced guard, the vanguard, and they are not concerning themselves with more than clearing the vicinity of the road. To right and left of the track you may see possibly as many as four or five small bodies of men, each arranging within itself to cover movement by fire, and all climbing as rapidly as possible towards points commanding the line of march. Flank piquets moving out. Fairly close behind the vanguard is a conglomeration of troops. You may see a section of guns, trails on the ground, preparing to open fire if any one of the piquets is opposed. If you do not see these they are probably a mile or more in rear, and in that case you will see guns moving up fast past the column, leapfrogging their other sections in action and coming up, to down trails as far forward as possible. You should also see a body of men in some sort of loose fighting formation, either moving forward, or, if halted, prepared by its fire to help the piquets forward. This is the main guard, never used for flank piquets, but kept intact for its job at the end of the march when it supports the vanguard in clearing the ground selected for the night's halt and its vicinity. There will probably be machine guns in readiness, possibly ranging on the various points which the flank piquets are approaching. Altogether a busy little scene.

At their head and somewhere off the path will be a small group, mainly officers, in earnest confabulation. These are the advanced guard commander, his staff officer, the commanding officer of the battalion supplying troops for the flank piquets (unless, as most often happens, he himself commands the advanced guard), one of his company commanders, and one of the latter's platoon commanders. Close behind is a platoon, obviously awaiting orders, while behind them you may see a couple of platoons or more moving up past the main guard to take the place of the waiting platoon which will shortly move off to take up the piquet or piquets entrusted to it. Close behind the troops of the main guard comes what is obviously a formed column of infantry, the balance of the piqueting troops.

So far you may see these people reproduced in ordinary training, but now you strike something out of the usual run. Behind the piqueting troops you will see a small body of men with a lot of mules under load, looking rather like a pack battery without guns. These are sappers, and perhaps a company of pioneers or what is left of them, for they have dropped the groups of men you see working like beavers away back on the track improving it for the transport. They may have dropped the greater part of their strength if the spot where you came on the column is more than half-way through the intended march. Next these is a Red Cross flag—just a dressing station's personnel for no bearers are needed here. Then comes a small party with a dozen mules or more under bulky loads, pumps and canvas sheets and what not—the water party, ready to develop the water supply on reaching camp, and very important people. And then the camp colour parties, also very important people, for their job is to get camp laid out and ready for the main body to march in without delay, and get on with their work, of which more anon. They are generally recognizable by their coloured flags, a bright patch in a dull landscape.

Further back along the track you see the main body —the first troops to look normal—the column commander's headquarters with its flag, followed by the fighting column closed up as tight as the track will allow, and behind them if you can see so far, and perhaps I ought to say, if you can see round corners, comes the transport. In the old days this used to be unwieldy enough, but as I have already said, what with masses of fully equipped ambulances, and increased rations (heaven knows how the human frame can stand the strain of the British ration), and heavier gun ammunition, larger small-arms reserves, wire, grenades, and so forth, which my younger days were not afflicted with, the transport column now is a huge thing and a nightmare to a column commander. The immensely improved transport organization of the present day has done something to lessen its road space, but you will often quote as you suffer from it, Kipling's " everlasting waitin' on an everlastin' road for the commissariat camel and 'is commissariat load." However, before you look for the transport, cast your eye along the hills flanking the line of march, and you will see small parties crowning the more threatening of them, and not, as you might expect, in neat little breastworks of stones, but sprinkled along some thirty yards or so of crest in groups and generally marked by a small coloured screen. Further down the slopes, almost always where the piquets are some distance from the road, you may see supporting groups, small in most cases, but as large as a platoon in others, while occasionally a small group appears, the company commander and his satellites moving back along the piquets he has put up, studying their lines of withdrawal, and preparing himself for the bad part of his day's work.

What you have seen is the normal appearance of a force marching in the hills without much opposition. The column is slowly moving past you; periodical halts and other checks ahead make it a desperately slow business. Still, it is moving along. Transport closes up at halts, not much help to the animals, but every shortening of the column, even temporarily, is to the good. Along the line of transport move little formed groups of men, six or so in each—the baggage guards, and behind each battalion's baggage a dismal group of regimental followers. A sad little push, and small blame to them, for they get little enough fun out of these shows, and little sympathy from the old soldier in charge of them.

You should by now be seeing occasional formed bodies—a party of sappers or pioneers, their road work done, and moving up to their heavy work ahead, or a company of infantry marching as rapidly as possible up to the front. These are piquet troops withdrawn and sent abroad by the rear guard commander, if he is not pressed. Somewhere you will see a section of guns or more, trails on the ground and facing to the rear—these are part of the guns detailed to the rear guard, which no rear guard should lack.

By now also, the camel transport carries more regular loads; the ammunition column is in front of the ambulances and the troops' baggage but the supply column in rear forms nearly half the mass and has its guard of at least two platoons, marching in formed parties along its length. And behind it comes a little body of infantry, a weak company or a couple of platoons, closing up the transport column; and guarding all these helpless animals, apart from their immediate protectors and helpers, is the network of piquets and supports holding the hills from which sniping would otherwise be continuous and the ravines and other lines of approach down which rushes in strength are to be feared.

At first sight it seems as if some sniping must be possible. It is, but the sniper hates being killed, and with the countryside overlooked by the protective parties he is always in fear of it, and that is what makes the system effective. I take much pride in the fact that except at the Ahnai Tangi where transport had perforce to be brought close to the fighting, no transport animal or attendant was killed on the march during the operations of the Derajat Column.

Well, the column moves on, a continuous stream of armed men, in large or tiny groups passing from front to rear all along its length. Now comes a little space, and you see troops in the valley bed and on the flanks, but close in to the track and obviously disposed for fighting. A group of ambulance ponies, and stretcher-bearers with a Red Cross flag (to distinguish only, for the Red Cross, if it does anything, only enrages these sons of the Prophet), a line of men in action in a fire position, with two or more other lines supporting them or on the move to a fire position further back, with a section of guns perhaps just limbering up for a leap-frogging move of three miles or so; machine gun sections at suitable points all prepared to help the piquets off and assist the rear guard; and a group of men, officers mostly, somewhere close to the supporting troops and watching both the rearmost line in action and the piquets on the hills. This group is marked by a large flag, usually red, a little distance from them. Watch the group.

One of them is following the movements of a piquet which has vacated its position, and is moving fast towards him. This is the company commander with the road sentries of that particular piquet. Near him should be more men, company runners, signallers, and escort. You see him turn towards the group of officers, acknowledge some order, spring to his feet and signal with a large flag towards, say, the left. He is calling up the next piquet to withdraw.

Now watch that piquet. If you had been watching half an hour back you would have seen part of it moving quietly down the hill to some point three hundred yards from the piquet or even less, and perhaps a mule scrambling down to the road. But now, the signal having been acknowledged, there is more stir in the piquet. Men in ones and twos slide backward and then nip off down the hill, gathering in little groups as they get further down and making for a prearranged point evidently behind the supporting party already in place. The men keep dribbling over the skyline, and it is impossible to tell how many are left, but no supporting fire can be given lest a casualty be made, and there is nothing more trying to the nerves than this watching men streaming away and not knowing when the stream is to end. All of a sudden some three or four men come over the skyline and dash down. When will the guns open? And the machine guns? Then, half a minute later another group slips over and comes bounding down, one of them waving a small flag or his helmet—the piquet is clear, and immediately a burst of bullets from the supporting party sweeps the crest and flanks of the slopes where the piquet has been. And next moment a swish of machine gun fire from the valley and perhaps a burst of firing from a near-by piquet or support, and then a couple of crumping shells on to the piquet position, and the piquet is safely started on its return. You can now look again to where fighting is in progress by the rear guard, but a later glance shows you the piquet collected and moving quickly up the line of transport after its comrades relieved earlier in the day. Meanwhile, the rear guard continues the withdrawal, its moves co-ordinated with the withdrawing piquets and its flanks to a great extent protected by their movements. The rearmost line moves back swiftly through its supporting lines, and leapfrogs into a position behind them, in turn to take up their work as they pass through. And so on and on through the weary day till camp is reached, or till, possibly, the rear-guard commander sees he cannot get in, and so determines, in good time if he is wise, to collect the piquets round him and stay out for the night.

CHAPTER IV.

Aspects of Work Falling to Junior Officers on the March.

Work with the Vanguard; and with the Transport.

LET us descend from our eyrie and take up one by one the duties falling to various junior officers with the column we have been watching.

* * * *

No need to enlarge on the work of platoon or company commander with the main guard or vanguard. The ground has to be cleared, and as soon as an enemy is suspected, fire and movement combined to get all forward with as little loss as possible, except to the enemy. The pace is really set by the flank piquets—by the delays in detailing them and by the slow process of getting into position. But those in the valley must not delay till these flank piquets are actually in position and ensuring a safe passage for the advanced guard, but must push on as soon as the piquets are launched and far enough forward to be able to assist the vanguard by spotting ambushes and by fire from above if the vanguard is attacked. Even this may be a counsel of perfection for if the advanced guard checks till it is quite safe for it to get ahead, it has failed in its job, which is to clear the road as fast as possible for the column, not for itself, to move in safety. This, I may say, is a principle which I have seen advanced guard commanders forget. When they do they have no right to grouse if they suddenly find the column commander a few paces to their left rear and looking devilish.

It is a difficult thing to gauge, though; if the vanguard gets ahead it may be ambushed as it was at the

Ahnai Tangi in 1920, and at Nili Kach in 1917, when the vanguard got ahead of two piqueting parties aiming at important heights. In this case the move was completely held up, in the former the main guard was at hand to help, and got it out, though with losses. I can only advise you to watch the piquets going up, and try to keep two or three hundred yards ahead of the main guard and in touch with it. You will find the main guard halts frequently once piquets begin to go up, for minutes at a time, sending bunches of piquets off at each halt. Use these minutes to scout the vicinity, and never move in dangerous and intersected ground without arranging for close covering fire within the vanguard.

The vanguard will more often than not move without opposition beyond sniping, for the enemy are not usually out to spend time and ammunition in resisting the vanguard with the whole strength of the column close by and the heights overlooking them about to be crowned by piqueting parties. And if there is strong opposition, not merely an ambush, the march develops into a fight, possibly a dogfight of the worst description, when vanguard work is soon at a standstill. I have seen my vanguard, or part of it, ambushed at the Ahnai Tangi, and being pulled out by the rest of the advanced guard with its guns in action at 250 yards. But there the march had checked, and a battle was developing. It was not in the least what a vanguard has to expect, provided always that it keeps its eyes open and moves in accord with the progress of the flank piquets.

In fact, I cannot teach you much in this job beyond a warning that on your alertness depends not only the steady progress of the column, but, and very much, your own safety.

One thing—you can help a lot by sending back early word of any work needed on the track. Every minute counts if the sappers are not to be overrun by the troops, and if this happens the track isn't likely to be well prepared for the transport.

* * * *

The next job of the young officer on his own is with the camp colour parties, if he has to take the quartermaster's place for any reason. We will take this later, for his work begins at the end of the march. But there is another duty which had best be dealt with here before we get on to the important ones with piquets and rear guard. And that is the work of the Battalion Transport Officer.

Your battalion has animal transport allotted to it for the Mountain Warfare scale of operations. Some animals, of course, are always with it—the machine gun and Lewis gun mules. But with these the transport officer should have no dealings—they are battalion animals and the especial charge of those they help to make war. The animals which on service concern the transport officer, who, let us assume, is yourself, are the pack mules of the First Line Transport and the animals, mules or camels, of the train.

The first line transport of the battalion carries, usually, company small-arms reserve, grenades, pistols and lights behind each company; and behind the battalion signalling equipment, entrenching tools, water, stretchers and medical equipment, with the battalion reserve of ammunition. The object of this is of course for the companies to be complete with those things which are essential for their immediate fighting job. Other mules, what we used to call the " B " Echelon of the First Line Transport, carry cooking pots and a day's rations and greatcoats, or blankets if it is cold, and the men are carrying their coats. These are needed at once on reaching camp, as you will see later, and march with the transport column heading the camels. The balance of unit baggage is taken on the train, usually camel transport.

All these animals are organized in units, with their

D

own supervising personnel, but when they are wanted they are drawn by you as transport officer of your unit or by your myrmidons the transport staff of the battalion, and returned to their own unit at the end of the day's work. This ensures their being looked after by someone whose good name depends on their care. Usually the same transport is issued to the same fighting units for their daily task, and the same holds within the unit, animals going to the same company and to the same loads each day. This helps enormously and is liked by both attendants and animals, and particularly by the mules, which are fussy beasts. I remember the trouble a certain kilted battalion had in loading up for a march with mules which had met them that morning for the first time. The mules simply wouldn't let the kilt near them, and in the end, help had to be got from an adjoining Indian battalion, whose clothes the mules could understand. There was a good deal of friction at the beginning of the march, but less towards the end, and next day the sense of outrage had faded, and all went well.

Your task as transport officer of the battalion is to make friends with the transport units which supply you. Be as helpful and tactful as you know how, to ease the transport in their weary work, and by careful attendance to your own duties on the march, and at the end of the day do what you can to keep the animals fit.

Your first job on the march is to get your animals, except those the battalion has taken with it, properly loaded at the right time and started at the right time from their loading places to fit in at the starting point, with baggage guards properly distributed and your own staff detailed to where they can best supervise on the march. This means, of course, careful calculation, reconnaissance of the best way to the starting point and of the tracks from it to the main track; and this again means training and using your particular personnel in the same work, for you will not be able to do it all yourself.

Well, we have got the transport started. You now have to be on the move. In your place, I should ride on past your camels and catch up the mules heading the transport column. Yours being a good battalion, you will find the mules moving quietly along with two or three N.C.Os. and some twenty men marching on both sides of the mules in parties of five or six. Why in parties? Because it takes three or four men at least to lift and fix a tied-up load, and one to watch their rifles while they are doing it. And on both sides? To get at the loads from both sides without having to dodge round a string of plunging animals. The regimental followers, poor devils, march immediately behind the battalion mules. There should be a stout old soldier in charge, using his little brief authority to the full—it will be needed.

If the animals can move on a wider front than two abreast, see that the baggage guards march inside of the mass of animals as well as on the outside, as if there were pairs of columns of two abreast, so that men will be ready to help in the centre. If you haven't parties between the long strings of animals, no one will be able to get inside to a shifting load in time to get the animal reloaded and on into his place, and your double column will gradually string out and the broad front on which your column commander has been hugging himself will become the narrow one which means delay and all sorts of consequent trouble.

While on this matter of baggage guards, see that it is well rubbed into them that their job is not only to guard and adjust their own loads, but to help with any loads that are in trouble, the object, again, being to avoid delays. Your own men will do this, of course, being well trained in this as in all duties, but a bad battalion will be shown up at once by its baggage guards. I have seen more than one where help was given neither to other units nor to other companies of their own battalion, while the officers' batmen, joyful brigands all, cared for nothing but getting their own sahib's mule up to the front as far as they were allowed to go. You as transport officer must check this sort of thing, under the authority of the brigade transport officer, whose man you are for the march.

Having seen your mules, fall back to the camel column. The Indian Camel Corps organization is, or was at the end of my time, as nearly perfect as such a form of transport can be—far different from the mass of ill-treated and underfed animals and men which I began with—and you will usually find the camels plodding along steadily and well closed up, unless they have met their two worst enemies, mud and hairpin bends. Any kind of greasy surface, such as occurs after rain in fields, or in the approaches to fords, make the unfortunate camel do the splits, but this can be avoided by heavy work—sappers and others throwing reeds or pebbles or gravel steadily on to the mucky bit. The hairpin is far worse and is practically incurable. Take any hairpin bend you know and in your mind's eye recall its sharp drop on the outside and its steep though small bank on the inside. The first camel follows its attendant round, the second, whose nose rope is tied to the leader's saddle, cuts off a bit, and the third one as often as not stumbles over the little bank, jerks its head up and breaks the nose rope, which has to be easily breakable lest a good tug tear the nostril. The loose camel now stands proudly upright with his load, which stays on mainly by balance, slowly slipping off. And that means delay, however alert your baggage guards, for there is only one attendant to three camels, and the camel requires expert handling if he is to stay quiet. A man with a pole, to shove the camel away from the drop, will improve matters somewhat, but the camel, unless it knows the pole man, or the pole man knows camel talk, will shy off violently and then the nose rope goes. Altogether, a hairpin is the devil, and your " Q " Staff and the sappers who have feverishly made roads up into camp and off it, even if they have to work after dark, should see to it that there are no hairpin bends in these. But they may forget, and in any case an angle in the neighbourhood of sixty degrees will do the trick, and you may find these anywhere on the march—at fords, round rock corners, at ascents into cultivation—and you have to be ready for them.

I spoke of a string of three camels, but this is seldom seen, as the " sarwan " goes sick oftener than his camel at the start of a show, and you may have one man leading four camels or more. The string will often be much longer, for I have found that the best way to keep camels locked up is for the men to work in pairs, one leading the camels in charge of both, and the other man moving behind and encouraging the camels with the strange noises the " sarwan " alone can make. This keeps the laggards moving well, and relieves the strain on the nose ropes, and is altogether sound until a hair-pin is reached.

By the way, don't be misled into believing that the camel is an evil brute without guts, who lies down and dies just to spite you. I know a lot about the camel, and I know him to be a lion-hearted beast who will not lie down to die until he knows he is dying.

We will assume after all this that your camels are coming along well. Your brigade transport officer, to whom it was usual in my time for battalion transport officers to report for orders overnight and again in the morning, will have given you instructions probably of the " carry on " type, with a few points of march discipline to be watched, and your job is then best done by riding up the line to its head and dismounting to watch the animals file past. You may be alone, but there is little danger in this. The flanking piquets will keep off individual snipers or draw larger numbers to themselves, and the constantly passing baggage guards are there to calm down any lad who hopes to creep up and get a free pass to Paradise—but don't stray. Keep close to the column, where your job is. I lost one good friend whose modesty forced him to withdraw from the line of march without taking an armed man to watch him.

If there should come an attack on the transport column on the march, in any force, you and the baggage guards have an important job—and that is, first of all, to be ready to check at once, with bullet and bayonet if needed, any sign of stampede on the part of unarmed personnel, of the transport and others, which, of course, means a stampede of animals. And if there is a stampede—and I have seen two—it will hold up the march indefinitely and completely upset everything. Ever seen a camel with its neck out, all four legs flying and its load under its belly? Upsets the best troops.

And then you have to be ready to repel the attack if it comes on you. It will usually come in on the ammunition column, as being more worth while, and this should have its special escort, so will have a formed body at hand to act at once. But these attacks are less likely to happen now, because the tribesmen are better armed and prefer not to get to close quarters when there is small chance of getting out of them.

* * * *

You are by now getting along to the next halting place. Constant checks will occur, but though the animals with the fighting troops should be relieved of their loads as often as the probable length of check makes it worth while, you with the transport column will never be able to enjoy these. Far from off-loading, the baggage guards will hardly have time to look over their loads and adjust them. So halts don't do the animals much good, if any. I have seen efforts made by enthusiastic young transport corps commanders to park their animals at each check, with two results only—delay, and cursing from their more experienced seniors. The thing to do is to close up as far as possible, adjust loads, change from sick to spare animals if necessary, and " shahbash " the personnel who will respond to this better than to impatience. And push on again as fast as you can.

These two things—speed without haste and a well

closed-up column is what the Column Commander wants if he is not to be anxious all day; and an anxious Column Commander isn't a pleasant fellow at all, I assure you.

* * * *

The troops usually enjoy a halt at the end of each clock hour, apart from minor checks. The transport get no periodic halts. There is one long halt usually provided by the check caused by getting off the main line of march up to camp, but which if not so provided is still essential. And that is about half a mile from camp, to let the animals stale; the camel in particular—he is a smelly, messy beast. And the men, too, because they are not likely to be free for some time after getting into camp what with meeting their guides, getting to the unit area, unfastening loads, checking loading ropes, getting back to their own standings, reporting, getting orders for watering and drawing supplies, getting the animals into their standings—all these take time, as you can well imagine; and the wretched transport attendant is made like you, and has fewer people to tell him where the latrines are, even when he can get away. So see that he knows when he must break off for the last time before reaching camp. I remember well an incident of the bad old days, when the "drabbie" had fewer friends than he has now. One of them was hauled up before the Provost Marshal (whom the Indians more aptly called the "Bum Major") for leaking in a forbidden spot, and was promptly given half a dozen. I shall never forget that great red-faced blighter with an excellent tea inside him, ordering punishment of that sort to a wretched devil who, after all, had to make water or burst, and who hadn't been told where he could, and who had to march next day. Apart from the first sense of indignation it gave me for all time a sympathy for the transport men, which I hope has been some use to them.

As for the animals staling, the later they do it before

reaching camp the less they will foul the area of the unit they serve, or, and this is the unforgivable sin, the area of other units which they should have been led around and were not. However, enough of these intimate details. You see your own unit's animals safely into the hands of the guides who should have met them some little distance from the fast-forming camp, and yourself get off to your mess, have a snack, see that your men are helping the transport to collect their loading ropes, and then off to your brigade transport officer to see if you can help. Ten to one you can't, but he will give you an hour at which he will wish to see you in connection with the next day's work; and then you are free, if you are not spotted by the adjutant and caught for some other fatigue.

CHAPTER V.

ASPECTS OF WORK FALLING TO JUNIOR OFFICERS ON THE MARCH—*Continued.*

Junior Officers' work with the flank piquets.

Now for the duties connected with the piquets sent out to the flanks from the line of march, which are the most important and the most difficult falling to a young officer in frontier work. For you are quite on your own, with no one near to look to for guidance in a task on which in the last resort may depend the safety of the entire column and which in any case must be done well if sniping casualties are to be avoided. And you have a duty to your immediate command—to do the work with as little loss to your men as possible, not only because they trust their lives to you, but because casualties, apart from weakening your power, add greatly to your difficulties. So you will see that the more you know about this job before you take it on, the more useful an officer you will be, and the better will be your chance of coming alive out of it.

Before I begin, I should like you to compare the Manual with the following, which is one of Lumsden's training notes—I forget how old, but well before 1870.

" Flanking parties are generally left from the main column at commanding points, right and left of a pass, to hold the ground till the arrival of the rear guard, and protect the flanks of the baggage. The officer in command should have a slip of paper given him with his name, corps and strength of his party noted on it, which he will deliver to the officer commanding the rear guard on joining him. These parties should not, except on an emergency, be kept with the rear guard, but be ordered on making their report to rejoin their own corps. Thus a constant succession of parties will be found patrolling the whole length of the column of baggage ready to succour any point which may be threatened. The posting of these flanking parties requires much practice and judgment so as not to detach more than necessary and at the same time to ensure perfect safety along the whole line."

As I hinted before, not much change in sixty years from the system the Manual orders now. The only difference is that with the present armament of the tribes, practically the entire line of march is under fire, so the work is more important, and has to be more thorough.

The Manual deals very fully with the question, and with the method in the form of a training exercise, but there are some bits which will bear expanding. Before I go into detail, however, I want to rub in the need for full peace training. For all movement in the mountains, as I have said before, is attended by delays, unavoidable and unforeseeable, and this is more true of piqueting work than of any other. So we must do all we can to ensure that there are no avoidable delays, and much can be done in this way if all are trained to their job.

I am not going into the detail of an advanced guard commander's work. He is a senior officer and should know it, and if he doesn't he will soon be for it. So he will be wise if he speeds things up by looking ahead as far as he can, by having a clear-cut method of detailing the piquets, by supporting their advance by fire if needed, and by keeping the number of piquets down to a minimum. A difficult thing, this last, requiring lots of practice, and a good eye for country. And with all this, he has to steel his nerves and be ready to push on as he sees his piquets have reached, not the points they were directed to, but to where they can give reasonable help to the vanguard. It may even fall to the main body to give help to get the piquets into position, the advanced guard having passed on ahead; and this is certainly to be preferred to the dangerous delay which is certain if the advanced guard waits while its piquets get settled and shipshape.

I think I am right in saying that opposition to piquet posting is not likely unless a stand up fight is in the offing, and that the piquets seldom have much trouble in geting into position, except to cover camp. The reason is of course that there is no great chance of getting rifles from troops with plenty of time at their disposal and with a strong force at hand—at least, not one tenth the chance that the withdrawal of the piquets gives. And you will find that the tribesman, who, after all values his skin, will generally wait for the better opportunities offered by closing with troops who have to get away and who, therefore, cannot turn and overwhelm him.

It is not surprising—with well-trained troops you not only have portions of the piquet disposed to cover each other, but you have adjacent piquets helping with enfilade fire, machine guns in readiness and guns prepared to batter the hillsides—enough to breach a Hindenburg Line, much less scare off a few ragged desperadoes whose hearts won't be in it till dusk is nearer. But, if the piquets neglect precautions, they will meet an enemy sure enough, and if your battalion is ever marked down as a careless one, you may expect more trouble than most.

* * * *

Let us get on to the detail of the junior officer's work, and read and re-read the Manual along with what follows.

Two commanders in your unit are directly concerned in a piquet's task—the company commander and the piquet commander. Your company will have moved up from behind the main guard from its place in the line of march and will now be ahead of it, ready to split up into piquets as required. It may be that you, with your company, are told off to occupy a swelling feature or ridge flanking the line of march for a mile or so.

In this case you go up and distribute your command to hold it to the best advantage, yourself, if you are the company commander, organizing the withdrawal along the feature to conform with the rear guard commander's directions. This is a fairly simple matter, but it is not usual, and we will assume that the normal routine of posting flanking piquets is under way.

As company commander, your duty is to be handy while the advanced guard commander points out the position he wants held and gives his orders, which will usually be given direct to the piquet commander. Quite wrong, of course, to side-step the chain of command, but experience shows that it saves time and errors. You will take a sight over his " pointer staff " (see Manual) for your own information as well as a check, listen to the orders, and make out the piquet slip which the Manual tells you about. This saves the piquet commander's time, and you will see that he has lots to do with his. Then you will give the slips to the piquet commander, tell him where the piquets nearest him are aiming for, listen to his orders and prompt if necessary, see if the next two or three piquets can be provided by your company, pass word or signal to the next company if they cannot, and then keep a fatherly eye on the piquet as well as on those previously sent up from your command.

I suggest a notebook with details of piquets and notes of the best way to bring them off. It may be useful in case you are knocked out.

* * * *

Take it that you are a platoon commander. You are as likely as not to be in command of the next piquet to go up—let us make it so, anyway. Your men have moved up to the front of the main guard, and you yourself should be close to the company commander and the advanced guard commander so as to take your instructions and get off without delay. The latter gives you the position to be taken and the number of rifles for the task. You make a rapid calculation and pass word to your next in command to move off the track on the side the piquet is to be, either the whole platoon, or one, two or three sections to cover the number of rifles ordered. The advanced guard commander cannot tell you how many sections are needed, for he cannot tell how strong your sections are; and you cannot tell how many rifles are needed—the advanced guard commander alone can know what you may be up against, and, also, it is in his own interest not to waste rifles. That is the reason for this slightly complicated procedure.

While your men are moving off the track and up to you, you take the advanced guard commander's orders, look over his pointer staff, salute, and turn to your men. Pull out your own pointer staff (never be without one, for it leaves no room for the personal error as the ordinary ways of indicating targets do, and its uses are legion) make up your mind as to the best way to advance, rapidly explain the position of the piquet to the men and your plan for reaching it, and point out positions aimed at by piquets previously sent up.

Split your command into two portions. As soon as this is done, ground scouts from the leading portion should dash out and get ahead, the rest of the leading portion following at a good pace. The scouts should not get more than about two hundred yards ahead in open or easy country, far less in broken ground or steep slopes. Distance is got by the men in front putting on pace, not by the rear ones halting, so you have to be quick.

Take two piquet slips from your company commander, keep one and give one to your " road sentries," of whom more anon, and then you follow on with the rear party, not more than two or three hundred yards behind the front party, and preferably on a parallel spur to the one they are moving on; and your piqueting party is fairly launched on its job. The Lewis gun should be with the rear party, and there should be a pick or two, signalling flags, a stretcher, and if standing orders lay it down, as they should, a small coloured screen on poles, or the artillery screen (khaki on one side and white on the other) as used in India, to help those in the valley to spot where you are.

The ground scouts are now ahead, but not too far ahead of the front portion. When they get fairly close to the position or to any point where an enemy may be lying up, they take cover and wait for their friends. Somewhere within close range of the final objective the front party takes cover and waits for the rest to close up on them, and then moves on under cover of the rear party, which should be ready to open fire at once if needed. Now, do not forget, I mean at once, and that means not only ranges taken and targets distributed, but catches down and men watching, rifle cuddled into shoulder and ready to press trigger. And you and anyone with glasses, have these out and sweep the crest and its flanks, so that the moment a grey rag flutters it will be spotted and a bullet reach it. That is why close range is insisted on for this covering fire. If the enemy attacks, all you will see is a sudden burst of dirty grey lumps bounding down the hill at an incredible speed, while an equally sudden burst of bullets in your midst will delay return fire unless you are as ready to open it as I have said. And if you are not, probably all you will see after a few moments of unhealthy excitement will be one grey figure on the slope, with luck, three or four of your men knocked out, and two rifles lost, and no one's fault but your own.

Another point—the ground scouts must wait for the front party before the whole move on to the crest. As witness a famous frontier battalion's experience at Kharappa, in the Mohmand country in 1908. Taking up a camp piquet—scouts, four of them—were ahead of their platoon by some three hundred yards, and all were moving up the hill when the four were attacked, killed, their rifles gone, and the entire move held up till an additional half battalion had arrived from camp to take the hill. You see, apart from the loss, delay—which is what you have to avoid.

As I have already said, slackness in your dispositions will almost certainly be punished. If you show by them that you are prepared, the preparations alone are sufficient to frighten off people of the sniper type.

Well, you have not made these mistakes. Your rear party, ready in every respect, is covering the final advance. Your front party advances, splitting perhaps to move round the flanks if the position is on a well defined knoll, and as it nears the crest, the men fix bayonets. Not so much for use, though for that in part, but there are few things more visible than a sudden flicker of steel, showing the waiting guns and machine guns below that the critical moment has arrived, and all will be on the alert.

No one there, but beware of bunching on the crest. For, almost always, another crest rises close by, and from it trouble may come. I remember at the Ahnai Tangi six men being dropped with one burst of fire, which could not have been from nearer than eight hundred yards, because they bunched when leaving a wall they had been building for a night piquet. And a loss like this, apart from starting a heavy day badly, will be seriously against your getting away safe at the end of it. Train your men to take cover at once, cover from which they can see and shoot, leaving dead ground to be dealt with by special measures. And now, all being well, your second party, with yourself, comes forward, and your work really begins.

* * * *

But first you have a mental struggle to win. The crest in front looks threatening, the advanced guard commander only gave you the approximate position, and you have much left to your discretion—what about it? The temptation is all to go forward and take it. If you give in and get there, the odds are on another crest, and you are no better off, with several hundred yards further to go when you withdraw; and those yards out of sight of all outside support. So be guided by one thing only—does keeping the enemy off your present position safeguard the column sufficiently? If it does, your job is to make it secure, and not to go farther afield. Cover must make up for loss of command—nothing will make up for a clear and short withdrawal at the end of the day.

* * * *

Now for the holding of the piquet position. First thing is to send out a covering party, to protect you while settling in. It goes out with due care and preparations for covering fire to where it can watch the immediate front and flanks from cover. You may have to push out a party to overlook ground from which danger to the column may come—send it out with all the precautions you took with your piquet, and later, tell the company commander. He ought to know.

Then you distribute your party, all but the road sentries if with you, so as to cover as much front as fits with keeping them under your control. Each man throws up rough cover, or, better still, improves existing cover, which will look more natural to the enemy, who know your hill top better than you do. Do not bunch your men—death loves a crowd—and cover your flanks, for that is where the tribesman who means business tries to get round. Then take ranges, prepare range cards (if those useful things still have a place in your work), post one of your best men to keep an eye on the road and the rear slopes generally, collect some boulders to rock dead ground with, and then, the cover completed, man the defences, see that the rifles are distributed to the best advantage, explain generally to the men how you intend withdrawing, and then break off into groups, each providing a look-out man. Fix a place for the men to leak, etc., wide of the line of withdrawal, and then man the cover again, call in the covering party, and after a look round, make them break off to rest close to their posts, except for look-out men and a special man or two with glasses. And see that they do rest, and that you don't have what used to drive me wild at training—the whole piquet glaring over their rifles at a panorama of unbroken peace. Rest your men as much as you can, for in the very easiest circumstances they have a hell of an afternoon in front of them, with a hurried withdrawal, a march up a long column of transport, and a series of jobs awaiting them in camp. And in the worst case they may have a serious fight to stay and to get away, in which their own exertions are the chief factor in getting them out, a part in a long and dangerous rear guard action, and at the end, possibly, a hurried bolt into a village or onto a stony hill for safety during the night. So make your men rest. Not that they will require forcing in a few days, but the first few days are the ones to weather.

If it is winter, you may have to make them unstrap their warm coats—men don't like doing it, but on these hill tops the wind is like a knife, especially to the livers of heated men.

* * * *

Then come some more duties before you yourself can rest. Get in touch with neighbouring piquets, both on the flanks and across the valley. Then with your road sentries and a couple of good men reconnoitre the road you intend to withdraw by. Send the road sentries down to the track at the point whence the piquet started up, after pointing out to them the place you expect to come down. If you have to drop a small party for communication with the road, these have to sangar themselves and keep a sharp look-out all day. After closely studying the ground and your route, return to the piquet. This reconnaissance must never be neglected, and the sooner it is done the better, for you can then let your men know your detailed plan. They only know the way they have come up, say from the east, and you will want to withdraw in the direction the column is moving, and that, unless you are out for the day and join the column on its return, will be westerly. None of you have seen the slopes you are to withdraw over except from a distance, and these hills are deceptive things. Remember the Kapurthala piquet in '97 in the Khurmana. They started to withdraw down a route they had not examined, and part of them found themselves with difficult ground in front and the Orakzai behind. They were scuppered to a man though a strong piquet of good fighting stuff. And though other things contributed to the disaster, the trouble rose from lack of reconnaissance alone. And that isn't the only case of the sort in north-west frontier history.

Once your reconnaissance is done you can work out your plan in detail, fixing the spots where the first men to go are to stop to give covering fire to the rest. See that all know the piquets to left and right and across the valley, and then keep your eye lifting for your company commander, and you should be ready for anything. But it means heavy work, so when it is done, rest all you can, for much heavier is in front of you.

Remember, you are there till told you may come off. To be driven off, or worse, to come off without orders, while any portion of the force is trusting to your protection, will almost certainly reproduce the Shin Kamar trouble in '97, with probably far greater losses than occurred then, before your error has been corrected.

* * * *

I said awhile back, " the road sentries if with you." We used to call these " bayonet sentries," because they always fixed bayonets, partly for defence, but much more to mark them, so that the rear guard commander could pick them up at once. They are told off in pairs because that is safer; a single man may get heatstroke or anything, and fail of his purpose. Two schools of thought used to exist around these lads. They are first and foremost animated signposts, and as the news they carry is wanted by the rear guard commander as early as possible, I hold that it follows that they should be left at the point whence the piquet started, and that they should not go up with it except to make certain where it is. If they go up with the piquet and are then sent down to the point where the piquet intends to rejoin the road, they cannot point it out till the rear guard reaches the place where the piquet is to come down, and then, apart from the delay in calling it up, etc., to which we come shortly, the piquet has to arrange its withdrawal in a hurry, and even then the rear guard must inevitably halt for it. Delay—*anathema, maranatha,* and more so in a rear guard action than at any other time.

Some say the sentries should go up and stay with the piquet during the day. The Manual is clear as to the only time when this is necessary.

Some say the danger to these solitary men is too great, and unfair on them, and that they should go up and stay with the piquet for their own safety. If you have got into your head the appearance of a column on the march you will know that, far from being lonely, they are in the way.

Others say it is a waste of two men, and that the company commander should know everything, and be at the rear guard commander's disposal to point out his piquets. He will be, if the day is long and the distances short, but try to get round a company's piquets, and you will see that as often as not you can't return in time, and the road sentries are an additional safeguard against a piquet being overlooked. And not a safeguard too many, any rear guard commander in war will tell you.

So leave your road sentries (if your brigade training orders permit it) as a rule near the point where the piquet went up. Should the piquet's eventual position not be visible, they may have to go up and return, but their place is on the road before the rear guard commander gets there. You will generally have a man or two a little under the weather who will be fully fit for this duty but a hindrance at the top, where you want the men as fit as can be. Anyhow, wherever you have them, they keep one copy of the piquet slip, and if you are wise you will not let them keep it in a pocket where a sweaty hand may overlook it or pull it out with other things; or impale it on the bayonet, for a wind may blow it off and down the "khud." Make them stick it firmly in the headgear, or on the bayonet, but with a twig impaled above it. And warn them to watch the piquet and at the end to force themselves on the rear guard commander's attention unless the company commander has arrived.

Except just at the end, wounded from the piquet should come down early to them as the one fixed spot in a shifting world. This is better than making straight for the road, safer, and a known way. It also lessens the number of detached parties, for the road sentries can watch the wounded and release those who brought them down to return to the piquet.

That seems a lot about two signposts, but it is as well you should know. By the way, they do not count among the number of rifles which go up and which are noted on the piquet slip.

CHAPTER VI.

Aspects of Work Falling to Junior Officers on the March—*concluded*.

Junior Officers' work with the flank piquets, and with the rear guard.

WHILE piquets are busy on their hill tops, the company commander has his work to do. Get into his skin for a little. He has moved along with the advanced guard commander, helping to send up piquets and perhaps post a supporting piquet, until his command is used up except for his own headquarters, stretcher-bearers, and his personal guard. "Personal guard" sounds strange, with everyone on the alert everywhere. But remember that to do his work properly the company commander must be free to move within the line of piquets as he wishes, and a guard is needed. In my young days it was a battalion standing order that officers in action (we were few in the Indian Army and supervising rather than commanding companies, and therefore were a little separated from our men, as would be the company commander we are with now) should each have two men told off to be " on his right hand as shield on shoulder rides " with their bayonets fixed. Why? Well, if you had had a wounded man surrender and then leap in with a knife as long as your arm, to be bayoneted within three feet of you, you would not need to ask. And that is why my standing orders laid down that when dealing with a wounded or surrendered enemy those so engaged were always to have an armed man ready to act in their defence against treachery.

* * * *

Well, after that the company commander, when his command is used up, does as the Manual says. But he also moves along back towards the rear guard, calling up piquet by piquet to find out if all is well. He will have to wait a bit to hear from the latest to go up, and he may have to go up to piquets which seem to be in ticklish places and discuss arrangements for withdrawal and find out what help may be needed, but finally if he has time he lands up beside the first of his road sentries and waits there to help the rear-guard commander, from whom he takes over the actual work of recalling and superintending the withdrawal of his piquets from the time he is told to withdraw such-and-such a piquet till he has it under his hand.

And so the day wears on. You, piquet commander, are up in the cool on the piquet position. If very quiet you may send out a party (covering fire, remember) to look into any dead ground in the close vicinity. If very close—for instance, if your party is on the edge of a steep drop—rock the dead ground, to save your grenades till the end, and do not crane over for a peep, or the peeper may take it in the neck from the near-by ridges. Meanwhile, you keep an eye on other piquets and watch the track. Troops, mules, camels, all slowly creeping past; and when you see the camels carrying neat supply loads you know the time is near. You begin your dispositions. Send away any animals, occupy alarm posts, and then send away the Lewis gun and part of your command on the line you have selected for your withdrawal. Send with them the men who went with you to reconnoitre the way, with orders to drop men in doubtful places to guide the rest. This lot take up a fire position, inside close supporting range.

If the enemy is pressing in strength, you may not be strong enough to do this. If not, the same dispositions must be made, but at a great pace, when you get the permissive signal. If you have been pressed, enemy swordsmen are probably lying up just below you in dead ground. Rock this. In any case, rock it.

And then, as you see the rear guard flag approach your road sentries, give your piquet number by the age-old range method. Tens to the right, units to the left, or *vice versa*. I forget which. And keep on giving it. You may or may not get it repeated at once from below. If you do, cease, but don't cease to watch. The rear guard moves on, the flag very likely disappears behind bluffs, and so on, but at last you see it coming more or less abreast of you. Then you see someone—it may be your company commander, it may be anyone—signal up your piquet number again. Return the call and watch. Shortly comes the " Wash-out," or whatever signal is fixed in your Force Orders. It is bound to be a simple one. Why? Because any-one through his recruit's course must understand the range signals. But in these days of efficiency, why not by semaphore? Quicker and neater, and able to say more? Because you are at war, and anything may have happened to the semaphore expert, if any, with the piquet. Heat-stroke or a bullet, and no sema-phorist. And, lastly, why a clumsy thing like the rear-guard flag when there must be dozens of perfectly good flags, signalling, large—and small? For that very reason. Signalling flags will be fluttering here and there, but the piquet commander wants to know what to look for, and when he sees the old rear-guard flag stagger and halt and then begin to wave, he is really interested.

From now on the Manual is perfectly clear on the procedure. The " Wash-out," or whatever the signal, means " You can clear out now as soon as you like, and do it as quickly as you can." Acknowledge it and then do not delay. The rear guard commander cannot tell you when to clear off—you alone can tell what troubles are facing you. So the responsibility is left to you, but so is the obligation not to delay unduly. And do not forget—the piquet is not there to put up a fight and get honour and glory. It is there only to protect the passage of the column and you have been told to clear—the column is satisfied, therefore beat it as soon as you can.

By the way, I have seen a tendency in some quarters to maintain that a well-trained battalion need not train to the permissive signal, but that piquet commanders should be allowed to use their own discretion and come away when they see it is time. I am afraid this is an idea which could only have birth in the minds of those who have never been in a rear guard action. For, firstly, just as the rear guard commander cannot tell what difficulties face the piquet, so the piquet cannot possibly read the mind of the rear guard commander. He may be intending to stand and fight and to let the transport get away a bit; he may be intending to lay an ambush, which would itself be nobbled if the piquets covering it were withdrawing, and last, though by no means least, the theory does not allow for the bullet. The people in the valley may know that Havildar Thakur Singh, the best N.C.O. in the battalion, who is sure to be the next Jemadar, is in charge of the piquet, but for all they know he may have been quite recently " sent west," and Lance-Naik Tara Singh, the boob, may be in charge. And are you going to trust him to do what you might—I only say " might "—have trusted Thakur Singh to do? The " pros " are clear and may be excellent in theory; the " cons " are perhaps not so obvious, but they may all be facts and must be allowed for.

That is a long digression, I fear. Let us get back to our piquet. The Manual is clear—follow it and you cannot go wrong. But the picture may not be distinct to a novice, and without a clear picture in your mind you cannot train your men fully.

The first thing to remember is to give no inkling to the enemy that the actual withdrawal is beginning. He will know fairly well, for he has seen the piquets coming off one by one and if he has not seen the rear guard he has certainly heard it. Friends have signalled that the time is near and they will almost certainly signal across the valley when they see your men moving away. But if you keep your moves dark from him he will miss the critical moments, so have no exposure in creeping away. A difficult thing—the ill-trained soldier creeping looks like nothing so much as a wallowing buffalo, and you can spend a lot of care on this training in peace with good results in lives saved in war. Then you must try not to reduce the front held. At the same time, see that men are not left alone out of reach, for if such a one is hit who can get him away? And if the enemy is pressing, the men who are left must keep up the volume of fire. But note—*if* the enemy is pressing. At one time it used to be the fashion for the piquet to blaze away in any case just before it left. It would have done better to bugle the " Retire," yet these quaint ideas crept into peace training after every frontier show, ideas which ought never to have been thought of by folk who had done the work under fire.

As the Manual says, you name men to go off one by one. They creep backwards, get below the crest, rise and dash off just a little faster than they think they can. Then they catch up or slow down a bit and collect in little groups, still moving fast and now and then glancing behind to see if all are coming along, through or past the men lying ready to support and on to the next point you intend to occupy to help off the original supporting body with fire. Unless the distance to the road is short, in which case they take up position there and remain ready to add to the help the rear guard in turn is ready to give.

In all these movements the men must dash along as fast as they can, individual movement as rapid as possible, collective action deliberate and controlled.

Your piquet is now left with possibly three groups, fairly widely separated, and it is up to you to call back the most easily spared, and then the others. You have by now rolled up the " piquet screen," for there is quite enough activity on top for all to be able to see where you are, and no one can or will open supporting fire from below until they have seen your " All clear " signal. As you call back your last group, you dash off with them a yard or two ahead, all bounding along like young goats, but always with those glances behind you, and yourself with the flag which the commander of any piquet must hold, waving it vigorously in front of your body in the " Wash-out " signal. If you have lost your flag, then use helmet or head-dress or something easily seen. This is what we used to do and I like it better, as more urgently visible, than showing the screen as is now often done. In any case, you are responsible for giving that signal. If any men are left when you give it, no one else can be blamed if they mistake figures on the skyline for enemy, nor will machine guns or guns in the valley delay their fire. But, once given, it is up to your own support, some two to three hundred yards away, to see that no enemy come round your flank or over the top, and to do this they must be as ready to open fire as they had to be in the morning in the same duty. They will not open till they see an enemy or the grey flutter which is usually all they will see unless you make mistakes, for there is no use in making a noise and wasting ammunition from their position; but all must be on the look-out, glasses in use and eyes strained, to see that a chance is not seized and that you, who trust to them, are not endangered.

The guns and machine guns in the valley, however, cannot be expected to be so particular. If there has been trouble on the piquets, they will be ready, and as soon as the " All clear " signal is seen, bullets will hiss on to the crest and flanks, and shells will come crumping down, so make the most of your time and do not check for a moment till well out of the risks of short ranging.

Then, when you have passed through the supporting line, send on your last groups to the next fire position and yourself take charge of the line nearest the enemy.

You may have had casualties and have to hold on to clear them, or a counter-attack may be needed. Do not counter-attack for dead men if the enemy are in force, but you must get wounded off. And if you have to delay, let the rear guard know. Never forget this—it is not only very nerve-racking not to know the cause of delays, but it may be dangerous for you and for the rear guard. If you do have to counter-attack, and if you have to bring up men already in position to support you, leave the Lewis gun, to support and because it is heavy; and, your work done, carry on the withdrawal as before, only more quickly if that is possible.

Let us hope you have not to do it, but just carry on, your new front line withdrawing, but not in driblets, for that would now be a waste of time unless the enemy has come on and is closing with you. You pass through the supporting line and again stay with it while sending the rest on, this time probably to the road, and finally reach the road somewhere near the rear guard flag. You close to some sensible loose formation, check numbers, and report to your company commander or, in his absence, to the rear guard commander, who will move you off up the line of transport unless he is hard pressed and has to keep you to fight. You clear off up the line of transport as fast as you can, taking care not to stay with the little party which brings up its rear—it has its special job to do and does not need or like any other unit with it.

And so on to the night's halt.

* * * *

That is the most important activity which falls to you as a junior officer on the march and is the last we need discuss except those of a company or platoon commander with the rear guard. Here you are not in such a responsible position, as you will be acting under the direct orders of the rear-guard commander. The enemy may press hard, but all movement must be co-ordinated with the withdrawal of the piquets, or the process may become a dog-fight instead of a withdrawal. You may have to counter-attack on your own to get wounded off. This is a fruitful source of casualty and it may be of sacrifice, but it must be done, for you are fighting with men who, however fine their fighting qualities, are evil brutes when it comes to mauling the wounded and dead. The dead do not matter so much and they would be the last to expect others to sacrifice themselves to keep a dead body decently intact; but you cannot leave your wounded if it is in any way possible to get them off. Otherwise, do not counter-attack unless your rear guard commander so directs. He alone can judge whether it is advisable and he will only do it to relieve pressure and never for the joy of a scrap. For on him lies the responsibility of not allowing his part of the show to hamper the main operation and he cannot afford to waste time, and lives, in unnecessary fighting.

And this brings me to the ambush, which you will find advocated so freely. A successful ambush has a fine effect, but to be successful it has to be carefully laid, and if it is not in turn to get into a mess most careful steps must be taken to protect its flanks and to cover its withdrawal. And as the flanks can only be protected by the piquets, and as the rear guard commander is the man who deals with these, and as arrangements to cover the withdrawal directly can only be made by the rear guard commander, take care that no ambush is attempted except by his express order.

* * * *

Otherwise the rear guard carries on as in any form of war—alternate bodies covering those nearest to the enemy. If the enemy is pressing it will seldom be possible for all these bodies to be on the move at once. One or more will have to be in position ready to open fire. You can imagine that the rear guard has a trying time in any case, and that if there is much fighting you and your men will have all they want of movement and of strain, and you will be thankful when signs of reaching camp appear, even though these consist of prolonged checks ahead and of rising kick in the enemy. They will now do their best to get a chance before the helpless transport and their defenders are safely concentrated and the rear guard fighting may assume more of a back-to-the-wall character, until piquets covering the rear of the camp site settle into their positions and the rear guard struggles through, leaving parties to close the valley until relieved or until ordered to stay in position as camp piquets.

* * * *

Now let us turn to the work of settling into camp.

CHAPTER VII.

Aspects of Work Falling to Junior Officers in Taking up Camp.

Occupation of protective piquet positions by the advanced guard—Work of camp colour parties—Principles of lay-out and protection of a perimeter camp—Occupation of camp piquets.

Though there are not so many detached " subalterns' duties " in settling into camp, there are quite enough to try you high if you do not know them, and the first falls to the vanguard and main guard. You will remember that these were not used for the flank piquets; their job, apart from clearing the road, begins at the end of the march. For when the column commander thinks the column has reached as far as it is safe to go that night (he generally, if he is wise, settles this about noon, to give the miles of transport and his rear guard half a chance), he selects as good a camp site as he can, and the advanced guard commander, now that no more flanking piquets are to be sent up, starts with his advanced guard proper to close up the space between the two most advanced flanking piquets, and does it thoroughly. He sends parties up to seize any commanding ground from which the camp can be seriously sniped. These take up their assigned posts with all the precautions needed for flanking piquets, and may have more opposition if the enemy have tumbled to it. Say you are in charge of one. As soon as covering parties are out and alarm posts occupied and tested, ranges taken and so on, start gathering rocks, or if there is only shale to build with, filling sandbags with it or at least collecting it into heaps. Because these posts will all be held by night piquets, and if the occupants are from another unit it will be some time before they can arrive and so much nearer the night, when no man worketh—though he has to, as often as not, when the tribesman is out to fight.

Anyway, all that can be done to help comrades, of your own unit or another, must be done. Here you cannot do much more than build the piquet front wall, because you do not know what the strength of the piquet is or what its commander's ideas of his needs will be. But this work will keep you busy while you wait for troops from the unit supplying the night piquet or for orders to occupy it yourself. If the former, you get down to camp as soon as you can hand over, for there is always plenty waiting for you to do there; if the latter, much work is still to be done before nightfall and the sooner it is done the safer you will feel at dusk. But leave it for the moment till we see what is going on in camp, and in the apparent confusion of settling in try to find out what the junior officer has to do.

* * * *

You may have seen a plan of a perimeter camp. A neat square or oblong diagram, with transport, ambulances, supply and ordnance parks, and all the non-combatant folk massed in little squares and oblongs round two central streets. Guns, cavalry, sappers and possibly pioneers, also in neat spaces, and the whole surrounded by equally neat and straight but extended oblongs of infantry forming the protective perimeter.

That actually is the picture the " Q " Staff of the column should always have in their pockets, and that, in actual practice, is the camp you will never see in really broken country. What the Staff officer laying out camp does is to take his plan and in imagination pinch and pull it like the gutta-percha faces of my childhood till it fits the actual ground; and day after day you will find different camps assuming the most quaint shapes, though always fulfilling three conditions:—

The non-combatant units and camp reserves surrounded and protected by infantry on the perimeter.

Irregular faces so sited as not to threaten other faces, yet on a suitable tactical front.

Two wide cross-streets, one pointing in the direction of next move.

* * * *

As you suspect, a body of troops and transport disposed for the night like this does not in the least resemble troops disposed for the night in ordinary war. A column in this sort of war becomes, literally, a beleaguered garrison from dusk to dawn. Or perhaps more usually till the small hours of the night, for the tribesman is an individualist and is never prone to take on long night watches and possible dawn dangers for other people, and so sneaks off well before daylight to a little well-earned sleep and also to escape the attentions of the piquets, which will be looking out for intruders as soon as they can look out.

Of course your force resembles a beleaguered garrison because it has to be concentrated if the mass of transport and defenceless units is to be guarded, and it has to be behind protection because the enemy are quite able to pass between the night piquets during the darkest night and assault without any inkling reaching the camp till the uproar begins. So that the method of protection during the night which has been found best up to the present is to enclose the whole non-combatant mass by a perimeter, strengthened as far as time permits and held by armed men.

Normally, the enemy will not assault. He prefers to snipe and creep away before dawn. Also, the Pathan hates to fight in the dark. He dislikes death, anyhow, and dislikes particularly an unseen death in the dark, mainly because he is sure his many enemies will say he was not in the fight at all when he does not turn up after it. And yet assaults do occur, and sometimes do penetrate—Palosin in '64, Wana in '94, Malakand in '97, and one was due at Palosin again in 1919, but was fortunately stopped by the check and losses in the Mahsud assault on the Black Hill piquet.

So we have evolved and stick to the perimeter system of defence at night, in varying forms—and this will last till the enemy can use gun-fire or aeroplanes and until a suitable antidote to this has been found.

* * * *

But what the young officer is most interested in is in the laying out of his unit's part of one of these camps. Take a likely job for a subaltern if the quartermaster is ill. You may be told off in charge of the camp colour party, linesmen from each company, a spare N.C.O. and yourself. A wise battalion will not change men on this duty if it can help it, for a well-trained and accustomed colour party is the greatest aid to the unit and to the " Q " Staff. For, as in all things pertaining to this class of warfare, speed when the occasion arises is essential to success. In this case nothing is more wearing to the legs and backs of the transport, to say nothing of the nerves of the column commander and of the unfortunate rear guard, than delay at the head of the column while camp is being laid out, and it is up to the " Q " Staff officer and his henchmen in this activity, the camp colour parties, to see that not a moment is lost.

You will move along behind the main guard and the remains of the piqueting troops with the camp colour men and your colleagues from other units, drearily enough; but sooner or later you will see signs of intention to form camp. The column commander, or a " G " officer, or both, ride ahead to the advanced-guard commander. You should see considerable activity of piquets moving out to the front as well as to the sides, and as soon as you see the " Q " Staff officer moving up, catch his eye and get after him as quickly as possible, telling your colour party to follow at a good pace. You will catch him up in a comparatively open piece of ground; report to him at once. If he knows you for an old hand he will not waste much time in explanations. He will most likely merely show you

F

his sketch and say something like " That *gurguri* bush marks your left. Take from there two hundred yards due west and down the west face a hundred and fifty, to include the west exit, 3/102nd, on your left and 5/107th on your right," and off you go to the *gurguri* bush and start in. Incidentally, it is good business to learn and teach your men the various local bush forms. No better or more common aids to fire direction exist in a country where rocks are all the same colour and mostly the same shape.

Your party joins you. You pace one front of your area, dropping company colourmen on their sub-area, mark the angle of the camp clearly, pace down your 150 yards, marking the exit unmistakably, see you have joined up with the unit on your right (it should be the job of the unit on your left to join up with you), correct your company fronts if necessary, send the N.C.O. to meet and guide your unit to its area (do not forget this), and then you go off and report to " Q " and see if anything else is needed. You take orders about water, fuel, latrine sites, and so on. Most urgent of all are the latrine sites. The units behind your area are all dependent on these, and if fouling is to be avoided they should be dug and marked at once by men of the battalion sanitary detachment who should be with the camp colour party.

Meanwhile the company colourmen have marked out their area, and the lines of the necessary perimeter works. If I commanded your battalion, colour parties would carry ropes marked to show the front line of a ditch, a parapet, a firing-line trench, its parados, a support trench, its parados, and a two-yard-wide path behind that. A combination of ditch, parapet and trenches is usually the quickest cover to throw up, but if stones are plentiful a parapet with ditch in front gives better command and is best in wet weather. But some shelter against reverse fire is needed, and a rope marked as I have suggested will do for all cases. The main thing to remember is that if these preliminary markings are not completed at once it will be ten times more difficult to do it when the troops with their transport come surging on to the ground and start in to prepare for the next important thing—the making of the perimeter defences.

An area for the headquarter wing will be needed, so this must be marked out, and a place for the mess and main dressing station, and by the time you have done this your battalion, unless it is on rear guard, will be in and the company commanders carrying on.

* * * *

Now, before I go on I expect a criticism and a sound one. That you have a battalion with a front of possibly over three hundred yards with only about twenty-five yards of depth. What about the first principle of defence? Well, the extended front is to allow the few available rifles to cover the entire perimeter, and the restricted depth is to avoid taking up room which is needed by others, and as both these are necessary it only remains to mitigate the ill-effects of lack of depth by the best arrangements possible, and how? The column commander does his bit by retaining in the centre of the camp, close to himself and the cross-roads, a special camp reserve with which to expel the enemy if they penetrate, while each battalion keeps a small reserve in hand, and we shall see how depth within the unit is still further provided for.

I am a little hazy about the present battalion organization, but I take it there is little change in the company. In the old days we had eight companies each of four sections (really almost platoons, with twenty rifles in each) which changed later to four companies each of four platoons, each of three rifle and one Lewis-gun section, which was a very convenient organization for this kind of fighting except that the machine guns were weak. Now I understand you have three rifle companies made up as before and a machine-gun company, with a headquarter wing housing odds and ends with special jobs. Anyway, you can apply to the present day the principles that we used, using machine guns as well as Lewis guns to cover the perimeter with interlocking fire, and then with a little loosely thrown wire or other obstacles to give the automatics time to get into action, a few trip flares, your Very lights, and alert inlying piquets in the front-line trenches, infantry ought to hold an extended perimeter far more safely than ours could.

We set about it by telling off one company as battalion reserve and splitting our perimeter up into three sub-areas, each held by two platoons and the Lewis guns in the front trench, protected from direct and reverse fire by parapet and parados, and if heavy sniping was expected, by bays; two platoons being in the support trench, similarly protected and communicating with the front line by oblique covered ways. Trenches and parapet very shallow and flimsy, for there were never many men for work, but it gave protection against sniping, which gives confidence, inducing sound sleep. Officers slept with their men, those with no command had funk-holes made for them and for feeding in, guards were protected, and several dressing stations were made, generally in support trenches, for first-aid work and fairly deep, to allow, of course, of lights being used. The need for these was vividly impressed on me when our second in command, shot through the back at the Malakand, had to be treated in a well used night latrine, and when, two days later, a gallant surgeon had to spend part of the night under fire in the open holding on to a comrade's severed artery.

These arrangements give the depth we were looking for. At least, all the depth which can be arranged within a battalion, and it is satisfactory except that the battalion reserve may have a longish way to go to reach the flanks. And there is no reason why the perimeter should not be fully and safely held with a similar arrangement based on crossed fire of Lewis and machine guns.

Full earthwork or parapet protection may not be possible except in camps held for some time, for a front of some three hundred yards is hard to cover with two lines of trench in the short time and with the very few men available. But a series of short section or platoon trenches, provided Lewis and machine guns are well arranged and they have supports in close touch, trip wires covering the gaps, and alert lookouts, ought to be adequate for the first night.

But never omit the cover, however hurried. I remember, in the Mamund country, the Guides, old timers, were starting, as you should start, straight away at making cover. Asked why and told there was no need to harass the men, the C.O. played the idiot boy, said it was a regimental custom and did it matter, and went on at it. The other battalions thankfully desisted, and within an hour heavy sniping opened and they were digging literally for dear life with their bayonets, which in those days were triangular, and bad entrenching tools.

In those days an attempt to secure more depth, or at least earlier information of an assault, led to outlying night piquets being placed round the camp at, I think, Nawagai, with orders to come in if danger threatened, " waving the head-dress and shouting ' Piquet.' " Incidentally, this had been tried and had failed at Wana, and naturally, seeing the swiftness and silence with which the Pathan moves in the dark. However, in this case, the sole survivor of the British infantry piquet can be quoted. " Piquet? I'm the bloody piquet! Came in, I did, calling ' Piquet! Piquet! ' with an 'undred of those bastards after me, and you sloshed my bloody arm off ! " From then on the outlying piquet has not been in favour. If you have to use them, see that the piquet is sangared and wired against assault, and specially guarded against fire from the perimeter, and that your men are equipped to stick it out, but never let them run in shouting " Piquet! Piquet! "

You may come into camp so late that no perimeter, even a broken one, is possible. Then you must scrape up what you can or risk a broken night, because it requires a very hardened or a very sleepy warrior to hear sniping, know himself without cover, and sleep happily. It is as bad as being sniped when bathing. But in any case, mark the front line clearly with bushes and stones if possible, and if that is not possible see that you and your men sleep feet towards the perimeter line. Why? When a man starts out of sleep he naturally rises the way his feet are pointing.

* * * *

I said you might have very few men, as they would be wanted for other duties. Here are some of them. A well-run column will have called for a permanent provost establishment, a permanent supply column guard—not an escort, but a guard which knows the normal lay-out of the supply column in camp, the followers who belong and consequently those who do not—and a permanent water piquet, N.C.Os. and men who have the important duty of keeping order round the water in the trough and in tanks. Your unit will also be called on for brigade runners, signallers with the supply column, the ammunition column, and ambulances, and for brigade orderlies (a wise brigade staff will insist on at least one orderly sleeping at their office). It may have been detailed as battalion on duty, and that generally means, at least, a column headquarter guard, a brigade headquarter guard, one for each field ambulance, and probably a water-pumping party.

Then within the battalion your company will have to supply its ration parties, water parties, orderlies, and its share of the normal daily duties. Again, you may have had a platoon told off to escort the ammunition column, or the supply column, and you will have baggage guards with the battalion transport, and you should have thrown out at once on arrival in camp and before any work is begun, a couple of sections from the platoons destined for the front line to act as covering party till the defence preparations on the perimeter are complete and the alarm posts occupied. And when they come in a small piquet must mount till dusk over the day latrines lest any of your men be caught with their trousers down.

All this means a big drain on the workers, but worse is to come. As soon as your battalion reaches camp, an officer reports for orders as to camp piquets. Your battalion will have to find the piquets on its own front or most of them, three or four at least. If your C.O. is wise he will do what he can to speed up the occupation of these piquets and at the same time do what he can for the comfort of the unfortunates composing them, even at the expense of an early completion of the perimeter. I have found something on the following lines to work well. If there is a reserve company, it has less to do than the others, so two of its platoons find the piquets. All who are for the duty settle down at once to feed heavily and cook rations for next day, then fill up with water, in bottle and reserve, ammunition, tools, waterproof sheets, and blankets if cold, and with Very pistol and lights, grenades, sandbags and signalling kit, and start off to their posts. Meanwhile as many as can be spared from the rest of the company, with the company commander and good understudies to select the piquet sites, have gone up with full precautions and with ample tools and material, and there collect stones, fill sandbags and build the " sangars " (for these piquets have to be well prepared for all-round defence, unlike the day piquets you sent up on the march), stake and wire them if the enemy are in force, and generally do all they can to lighten the task of the real piquet when it comes. They also note the ground and the best way up to the piquet in case they have to relieve or reinforce it in the dark, for the work will fall to them. Then the real piquet garrison arrives, relieves the covering party (never forget that covering party in any act of frontier war), and the workers go off down hill to begin the many bits of work waiting for the reserve company, such as their own cover, funk-hole for the mess, cover for guards and followers, filling in holes, marking battalion paths, and so on. No rest, you see. If there is not a reserve company from which to detail piquets, or if it is not strong enough, one of the front-line companies must be drawn on, and will only be able to hold a proportionately reduced line.

By the way, in my young days, when the enemy had less offensive power, we used to send up small piquets, often just with greatcoats and ammunition. The wretched devils spent a miserable night, mentally and physically—it was most unfair and small blame to them if they were jumpy. Now they are generally strong, and should always be well protected and well found. It pays.

Now you see what I meant when I said there would be few enough for the work to be done; and I wonder if you have seen what it took me some time to grasp—and that is the need, before the march begins or at all events before arrival in camp, for telling off your command for the work which you can foresee will fall to them on arrival. Adjutant and quartermaster can help hugely in this, so enlist their aid. But if you do not have some system in the battalion the confusion and shouting will be awful. Try to let every man know before he starts whether he is likely to be for guard, covering party, watering party, or piquet or whatever you can foresee; and if each on arrival in camp gets ready to tackle his job you will save no end of orders, and time, which in camping arrangements means comfort, which spells efficiency.

You may be with the companies told off for column reserve. As a rule, the infantry escape this; the Sappers and Miners (the Indian equivalent of the Field Company) being indicated for this work. They are, to begin with, heavily officered, and they have had a heavy day's work on the road, are probably working till dark or after on exits and so on, and they need all the rest they can get, and should certainly not be on the perimeter. If the column commander can do without the pioneers on the perimeter he will add them to the reserve for the same reasons. Guns have their own job to do, and cavalry, if there are any with the column, have enough to do in a night attack in keeping their horses quiet and their own area clear. Still, if a body of infantry is needed and you are of it, your duties as a platoon or company commander are easy. Once the camp has settled in, patrol it thoroughly with your section leaders, find out where everything is camped, and do it again after dark; and, finally, warn your men what may have to be done and that if called on bayonets are to be used in dealing with any enemy met with. The reason is obvious, but the order is sometimes forgotten.

* * * *

Back to real work. Let us take it that you are in command of an important camp piquet. You have gone up with the advance party, you have occupied the position and ground ahead of it with full success, and started on the piquet defences. The Manual is very full on this important matter, and I can only add that special care must be given to making a covered loophole through which to signal, piercing the rear face diagonally if possible, otherwise blinded, and aligned on the battalion signal station. Without it, your piquet will be easily cut off from help.

Low loopholes are only permissible in a flanking bastion and even then are a danger; and are in any case hard to provide. The hand grenade has solved most of the former difficulty of dealing with a close enemy approach, so avoid the low loophole if you can.

If rocks are plentiful, much of the defences will be finished by the time the piquet troops arrive with all the impedimenta already mentioned. They are all necessary though an infernal nuisance, as in the morning all have to be sent away in time to load up. Water is the most necessary. Not only must you have water for the night and the early morning, but your men must start with full water-bottles. To hold all this, most experienced units have a canvas tank per platoon, holding twenty gallons or so, called a "diggi." This hangs on a collapsible frame, packs and mends easily, holds a lot of water and keeps it clean and cool. In the hottest day beer kept in it is as if iced. In bottles, of course. Your unit should get them if they are not by now articles of issue. Anyway, with a diggi or without, the piquet arrives. It must aim at starting at least two hours before dark to let the workers or the relieved piquet get back by dark. It relieves the covering party, puts away its impedimenta, and falls to completing the defences. Irregular head cover, preferably of sandbags, is really essential, as the sniper then does not know what to fire at, and if he has friends using covering fire your men can deal with both on even terms. Clear away bushes up to thirty yards or so—bushes in the dark have a habit of crawling about and even of speaking like Pathans, and your sentries will see all sorts of bogies unless you remove them.

The defences finished, call in the covering party, block up the entrance, fall in all on their posts, tell off into three reliefs of which one stays on the alert and provides sentries, at least one to each face; and the others should rest at once, sleeping at their posts, you yourself by a sentry. But before the men drop off, warn all that the men in the camp need rest, and that you are there to help them get it, and that jumpy sentries and indiscriminate loosing off of grenades and lights are not looked on as showing zeal. At the same time tell sentries to listen rather than look, and to take action on the least sound of stone shifting. A favourite trick with these people is to creep up and dislodge an important stone, bringing the parapet down with a rumble, an attack being made on top of the confusion inside. Be alert but not jumpy, or the object of the piquet is half-destroyed. Those who were with me at

Dakka may remember a hideously disturbed night when a piquet on the western ridge gave us a Brock's display lasting from ten to three, to find at dawn that no enemy could have been massing nearer than two hundred yards off. A short calculation showed that in that one night the young officer in the piquet had loosed off as much in cost value as was spent on his military education. It is a difficult thing to avoid all the same, and I can only suggest that you sit up for tiger or panther as soon as you can to learn how to give proper value to night noises and sights.

In any case, the Manual gives wise advice. Do not send up a light till you have good reason to suspect an enemy's close presence and until you have made arrangements to loose off at him when the light goes up. You may have errors even then, like the Mahrattas of a certain good unit who obeyed orders like men, and loosed off at the thing which had been forcing its way through their wire. Thank goodness it was only a donkey—had it been a cow, Lord knows what would have had to happen in the way of expiation.

While on this matter of noise round piquets, conglomerate hills are apt to spit out stones during rain, and cause alarm. The heavy rain after the Barari Tangi was forced led to a lot of this, and though the day after the fighting had been quiet, the night brought rain and slight slippings of the hill-sides, which so put the wind up piquets and perimeter that seasoned though the troops then were, the noise was trying and the waste of Very lights and grenades deplorable.

* * * *

By the way, I might as well tell you that taking up a camp piquet may not be such plain sailing as would appear from what I have been saying. It may have to be done under heavy sniping and even in face of assaults. In such a case, you will be helped by gunfire and by reinforcements from camp, but in the last resort you may have to hang on, pushing up stones in front of you to give some sort of cover till dark comes, and it may be easier to improve your hold. The Barwand piquet in 1917, which I shall have to mention again, the Flat Head piquet in the Ahnai Tangi, and the Gibraltar piquet beyond the Barari Tangi, both in the fighting of 1920, are all examples of what may have to be done to secure a position protecting camp. Whatever happens, nothing short of annihilation must loosen your grip on it.

However, let us hope the piquet is well and truly established and that the night passes without undue trouble. In the morning you either send off your kit as soon as it is light to take its place in the line of march, the piquet waiting till relieved by the unfortunates who are for rear guard; or, if the force is halting, settle down for a rest and clean up, awaiting your relief in the afternoon.

CHAPTER VIII.

ASPECTS OF WORK FALLING TO JUNIOR OFFICERS IN TAKING UP CAMP—*continued*.

Occupation of perimeter defences and subsequent work—Occupation of a village in emergency—Points to be guarded against in camp—Sniping—Assault—Daily Routine.

Now take the place of one of your comrades, down in the rapidly settling camp. Here, more than anywhere, good interior organization tells. Ever since the troops came in, except for short breaks for hurried snack or drink, they have been hard at it preparing the perimeter defences. Each company took up alarm posts before work began, and piled arms close behind their alarm posts under sentries who keep an eye lifting towards the covering parties. As many men as can work freely concentrate on the front line, ditch and parapet and trench, finishing this as speedily as they can, and then turn to support trench, dressing stations, and cover against reverse sniping. Then they spitlock or mark clearly paths within the company area, fill in holes and level lumps—very necessary this for free movement in the dark. The reserve company, or what is left of it after supplying various fatigues, makes cover for itself and for officers not with companies, marks paths, fills holes and levels uneven bits in the battalion area, and runs up some sort of obstacle, at the angles of the camp first and then along the perimeter if time permits. Bushes and scrub should be cleared for a good distance from the perimeter, to lessen cover for snipers and also to make the sentries' work less nerve-racking; but it is not a bad thing to leave a few bushes as an attractive screen for snipers to collect behind, to be dealt with by rifles in night rests.

Company mules have been off-loaded, and loads collected in rear of the company, and the mules have cleared off to their transport unit. In the case of all first-line mules, baggage ropes are kept, and loads always well roped up when not in use. The camels of the train are now sliding in, and these are similarly off-loaded handy to their companies, and sent off as quickly as possible, for they also have a lot to do before they can be settled down for the night.

As work proceeds officers have learnt the routine orders which affect the men—defence precautions, guards, police bounds, drinking, bathing, latrines, when the day latrines close and the night ones have to be used, ration hour, and so on.

* * * *

When the defence works are ready, arms are taken up, trenches occupied, sections in the front trench take ranges, covering parties come in, ammunition is made up, the full complement of company reserve ammunition, tools, water " pakhals " and filled " diggis " are placed *in* the support trenches, bedding is recovered and distributed, and night latrines prepared. Orders are given out, such as have been passed round. Then, a third of the men in the front trench are told off for inlying piquet, to provide sentries and remain in constant readiness, equipped and accoutred, in the firing trench. The remainder place rifles and accoutrements in the section trenches, and then prepare bivouacs or pitch tents. Always parallel to, not vertical to, the perimeter, to let men dash out from both ends in case of an alarm.

Then all but the inlying piquets break off, some for duties within the battalion, and others to wash, clean up, and rest till food is ready. And I think that one and all, junior officers as much as any, will agree to call it a day.

* * * *

That is more or less how matters go if all has gone well or as well as can be expected. Camp has been reached in ample time, piquets have been occupied, and the transport has come in, and the normal routine has been possible. You can imagine that in proportion as things go wrong, the march delayed, the transport held up, the piquets heavily engaged—by so much the preparations have to be hustled and the troops wearied and harassed if the essential work of defence and feeding is to be carried out. With good interior organization, difficulties will be frequent enough; without it they will be insuperable; but the blame will lie and the discomfort and danger will mainly fall on the unit which deserves it.

If everything goes wrong and the rear guard cannot get in and has to stay out to draw attacks on to itself and away from the transport, then much more hurried steps must be taken by it; and for its night's halt the outer line of piquets will in all probability have to be dropped altogether. This is one of the occasions the Manual foresees when it speaks of using a village for the night. The rear guard will be lucky if it has a village handy to dive into, for there it will find not only defilade but a good deal of protection from plunging fire. The book lays down, rightly, that troops should not occupy the village itself, but rather a perimeter outside it with room for movement between perimeter and village walls. Otherwise communication becomes difficult. And also, if an attack gets in, the villagers themselves are the enemy and know their way blindfold —having the perimeter outside denies them this advantage. But the perimeter outside is often a counsel of perfection, and many a time small and large parties have had to crowd hurriedly at dusk into a deserted village and take shelter within its walls with the enemy pressing close. Then you must widen and straighten the main passage-way and make others through the village from hut to hut and enclosure to enclosure round the outer wall. This must be done at once, and even more urgent is the removal of inflammable stuff. The enemy know exactly where this is, and if they have any kick left—and in these circumstances of a pressed withdrawal they are bound to have their tails well up—they may be counted on to creep up and lob a torch or ghi-soaked ball of cloth or fibre on to where they know rick or thatch to be. It is sure to happen, for the enemy know that in the confusion among men and animals following a blaze and alarm of fire on a windy night there is a good chance of revenge—and rifles.

So guard against fire, fix alarm posts, make certain the ways to them are known, and so on. A useful booby trap can be made by loosening a foot or so of the top layers of the mud-bricks on outside enclosure walls over six feet high. The enemy leaps at the wall and grips the top, down comes the top with a run on top of the leaper, and it is disconcerting to have a few feet of your own garden wall falling on to your chest, to say nothing of what the roused defenders may do.

While on this matter of walls, train your men to keep a good grip of their rifles when using loopholes—it is an easy matter for a tribesman to lie doggo near a loophole and trust to a sudden grab and pull to give him a rifle worth to him some five hundred rupees, which is the equivalent of three wives or two really good cows, and so worth taking trouble for. You will find all the ground floor loophole plates on permanent frontier posts with holes just large enough to hold the rifle and allow of play, but not big enough to let the bolt and butt through, for this very reason.

* * * *

Wherever and however you get into camp, there is a most important point to keep in mind, that, in an inexperienced push—that is, almost invariably at the first entry into hostile country—there will be more than a tendency—an irresistible urge—to reply to snipers' fire and even to blaze off at noises or fluttering papers. The Manual is emphatic on the idiocy of this, but no matter, your men will do it unless you yourself see to it that they do not. We were starting our well-earned evening meal the night we settled into camp at Datta

Khel in 1919, when one shot came sailing in from the west, over a good battalion, good but new to the game. Instantly—it said much for their alertness—the whole west face burst into fire, and rolling bursts of musketry flew up and down the line and would not stop till peremptory orders reached the unit from my headquarters. You may ask what the officers were doing. Well, they also were new to the game, and to them this appalling outbreak of fire meant only one thing and that a night assault; one and all dashed to their alarm posts like lightning and battalion control was lost for the moment. I can laugh at it now, but I was in a towering passion then.

Sniping, one would have thought, must lose its effect with the high-velocity rifle whose low trajectory might be expected to carry any bullet which missed the parapet clean over camp. But the fact that it can be used from farther off produces plunging fire, and camps are also much larger and the bullet has time to fall somewhere in among men or animals, and in actual practice it is more damaging than the old sniping, so that we may be thankful that cost of ammunition sets a limit on it. In the old days anyone with a flask of cheap powder and a percussion musket or " jezail " could have quite a cheery evening sniping camp from a hundred yards off—gave the sniper a warm feeling of patriotism and did not worry us much if piquets were in the right places. There was a persistent old bird who accompanied our brigade up and down the Khar Plain in 1897, who had a duck gun and a bullet mould which turned out eight-bore bullets in pairs joined up by a little runnel of lead—just like a small dumb-bell, and made a noise like a bull roarer. We quite missed him when a chance bullet laid him out. But, ancient or modern, sniping must be met by digging down or building up, if only to ensure placid sleep; and for the same reason in no case must it be answered except by order.

* * * *

If there is an alarm, the perimeter look-outs put up

Very lights and if flares are used outside the perimeter they actuate them. Nowadays flares are useful but not necessary while the better and handier illumination of the Very light is available. We found, by the way, that on occasion the lighting of these flares brought on the attack if one was preparing, as happened at Nawagai in '97. The inlying piquets open fire if this is needed, as do the automatics on the perimeter, and all the front-line troops, if in the trench as they will usually be when with the fighting column, rouse and join in repelling the attack. If in standing camp, they snatch up their rifles (these are never piled, but are kept in the bedding with the man if not buried beneath him with the sling round his arm) and dash out of the tents to the trench. Supports get into their trench, guards and reserves fall in, attendants and linesmen stand to the animals, all lights and fires are dowsed, and tents struck, the guns chuck up a star shell, and company messengers report at battalion headquarters if not already sleeping there, as battalion orderlies are at brigade headquarters; an officer from the column reserve reports at column headquarters, and, except for firing or fire orders, silence is aimed at though seldom attained.

If the attack penetrates, no one rushes out of his own area to repel it. The reserve spreads along the roads, isolates the penetrated area, and then begins the bloody business of dealing with the intruders with the bayonet by the light of Very light and star shell. A most unpleasant form of scrimmage.

* * * *

I do not think there is any record of an attack on camp breaking it up altogether—lack of cohesion on the one side and discipline on the other has always saved the situation; but it can be a very nasty show. The Malakand camp was entered in '97, though that was hardly a perimeter camp. The attack lost much of its force because the bazaar lay in the path of the attackers and drew off a lot, though many came on and had to be expelled at the point of the bayonet. At Wana in '94 the camp was well penetrated and we had a hundred and twenty casualties and a number of animals killed and wounded before the tribesmen were ejected. A lot of rifles were lost and no doubt the force of the attack was largely weakened by those who got rifles making off with them.

* * * *

When halted, as must often happen to get up supplies, put up permanent piquets, and so on; there is still much camp routine which cannot with safety be overlooked. First, alarm posts should always be manned by inlying piquets, strength varying with the unrest in the vicinity, an hour or so before daylight, or at the "Rouse" if the force is moving earlier. Dawn patrols are always needed within the piquet line. However prone to take care of himself the enemy may be, there are always some, generally elderly men, to whom the Prophet's Paradise holds out an allure so superior to the miserable life these people know, that they may well think it worth while to risk losing their lives, provided they can take an infidel with them. So it is not uncommon for attack to be made on unsuspecting men strolling about beyond the latrine and water sentries, trusting in the protection of the camp piquets. And the dawn patrol will rout danger out.

The hundred and one column and battalion fatigues have to be met, inspections done, roll calls held. All should use their alarm posts for falling in on, whatever the parade. A good battalion will always have a routine for the "Retreat" stand-to, when both trenches will be occupied, guards in their defences, Vickers and Lewis-gun detachments standing to their weapons, the battalion reserve in their cover, followers also, and men with animals standing to them. All men should be armed and accoutred, and all battalion animals saddled, and you should take this opportunity of seeing that your men are ready in all respects to move, with rations, water, full amount of ammunition and of sandbags and grenades, if carried, and first-line loads roped up and placed handy for loading. Then it will not be out of place to see that all have their cover adjusted to the fullest effect for night firing and protection, and that all have the orders so far as known for the following day.

Men should never wander about alone unarmed at any time of the day outside the perimeter, and armed men must in any case always be in parties, or the single rifle may be too much of a temptation to the odd Pathan risking death within the piquet line or even to the friendly Pathan coming in on his lawful occasions to the political officer. If the night latrine is outside the perimeter, it should be only just outside, and a sentry on the perimeter close by. Folk using the latrine must report to the sentry as they go out and come back, and, if armed, in this case leave the rifle with him. This is, of course, to lessen value as a prize and also, where the Indian trans-frontier sepoy is concerned, to check desertion. Officers should, of course, always carry a pistol when moving about, and by the way, if it is a revolver, never have more than five rounds in it, so that the striker may rest opposite an empty chamber. If it does not, as sure as God made little apples, some day when you are slipping your belt off the pistol and holster will slide off too, and if the hammer hits the ground first, one of your pals may " go west " in the rottenest possible way. In any case, you will get the devil and all of a fright and a first-class telling off. This is not far fetched. I have had a mule shot within a yard of me and a bullet between my legs another time, so be wise.

* * * *

A well-run column always has orders for keeping natives of the country out of camp. Some may have business with the political officer, who is always with the column in the capacity of Staff officer for political affairs—not as the supreme authority he used to be in the Afghan War days and even later. He will have a lot of work with those of the enemy who want to be friends, and these must have free access to him. They generally have to be seen outside the camp. Indeed, it is often advisable to have the political officer's following of friendly [*sic*] headmen, agents, spies, and so on in a separate camp or in a distinct wired-off part of the main camp. The spy, or "jasoos," is a quaint institution, whose conception of his duty is to take as much news to his friends the enemy as he does to his enemies the troops. A friendly sort of show, frontier fighting, till it comes to the actual killing. In fact, I have heard a most bitter complaint lodged by hostile sections that they had been denied the privilege and the emoluments of having some of their own men employed as spies.

Bar these folk, natives should not be encouraged, except to get them within killing range. For the innocent villager who strolls into camp with a chicken may be looking for a chance to knife or pistol some sahib, the bigger the better, for these people have sporting ideas about the big head, and there is no use taking risks. Risks which become greater as the tribe becomes more subdued, for that is the time for restoring hurt honour. It is difficult sometimes to spot them with the mass of Indian personnel of all kinds in the camp, but if you ever have to search, fall in all men in your area, order them to identify each man the man on his right and left and take them by the arm and step back four paces. If there is a stranger, he will be left without an arm-seizing friend, and you can proceed to investigate without loss of time.

CHAPTER IX.

ASPECTS OF WORK FALLING TO JUNIOR OFFICERS PUTTING UP PERMANENT PIQUETS.

Slow process of putting up permanent piquets—The operation—Dispositions to cover the work—The work—Duties after occupation and in succeeding days—The value of the system—Convoy escort duty—Dangers of the " Raghza "—The floating platoon.

A NIGHT has passed, and what is the order for the day? If an advance has been decided on there is a good deal of work for you, which I will take on in the next chapter. But if there is to be a halt, to replenish supplies, evacuate sick and wounded, and fill up for a forward move, you may be sure it does not mean a rest for you. The first thing a column commander will turn to will be securing his communications with his last camp, and as I have already suggested, this is best done by establishing permanent piquets to link up with those already put up from the former camp. And the next thing he will aim at is to put up more piquets as far in advance as he can, to ensure a flying start for his next move, and to secure his communications when moving forward.

The order for the day may then be what is known as " Putting up Piquets," one or more, the number depending on the troops available, their value, and the temper of the enemy.

And a most important and ticklish duty it is, for the troops covering it and the troops building the piquet, for the enemy are never in the least doubt as to what is to happen. They know that the troops covering the work have to get back to camp before dark, and that they must therefore withdraw at a known time, when they give attackers the certainty of the chance they are always readiest to take—attack on a foe who cannot retaliate beyond the most limited counter-attack. On the other hand, it also gives a certainty of more or less vicious fighting, in which the main object of the operations or what should be the main object—killing tribesmen—can be attained.

* * * *

Obviously, with this certainty of fighting, it is unwise to attempt more than is within the power of the available troops, and this in turn means that only a limited number of piquets can be established in a day. At first the number will be very limited—one or two in a day, if as many—but as staff and troops become accustomed to the highly specialized work, and as the enemy take knocks, the rate will rise.

To give an idea of how it can be speeded up, in 1919-1920 after the advance to Palosina, which was very ineffectively contested, it took eight working (and fighting) days to put up one piquet towards Jandola, and three forward towards Kotkai. At Kotkai there was a halt of twelve days, seven of which saw heavy fighting, and ten piquets established before the Ahnai Tangi, only four miles off, was secured and three more piquets put up in the two days following its capture. A three days' halt followed in the heart of the Tangi, during which time the enemy having had heavy losses, five more piquets were occupied before the advance to Sororogha. Here again five working days were needed to establish six piquets and prepare the forcing of the Barari Tangi. Thence to Piazha Raghza, only nine miles, nine days were required, with three intermediate halts mainly forced on us by weather. In that period twenty piquets were put up, six in one day. And thence to Makin required ten more days, twenty more piquets going up, though while actually moving there, seven piquets were established in one day, a tribute to the hard work and skill of the men and the grasp of the routine of occupation by battalion and column staffs. These figures hardly apply, of course, to normal operations employing highly-trained troops with all our latest aids. With war-weary men mostly ill-trained and new to frontier conditions, air equipment worn out and obsolescent, an inadequate artillery and no machine guns, speedier work could not have been expected. But the lesson remains—the need for organization on the part of commanders, from highest to lowest, and for will and power to work all out on the part of the troops.

* * * *

Now let us get ahead, as usual, with the duties of the junior officers with the various parts of the troops told off for this most unpleasant duty of putting up a piquet.

The troops to cover the operation will consist of a couple of companies or more—usually far more while the enemy have fight in them—with machine guns, probably under brigade control, and guns in readiness to support. The infantry will probably be started in the dark, to get a longer working day and for surprise, and make for their objective—ridges or crests covering the piquet position from some distance to its front and flanks, for the builders must have all the protection possible. The advance is not likely to be heavily contested unless the enemy mean to give battle, in which case the day's plans will have to be altered. But piquet protection gives too good chances to the enemy for them to waste their energy on opposing an advance when they know the advance must become a withdrawal at the end. So at first they will probably only harass both piquet builders and their protectors with long range fire, and thus at the first your job as company or platoon commander is a simple one—to take up and keep a suitable position throughout the day. But no slackness. An enemy may think it work while to creep up and rush a part of the line, covered by his friends' fire from far off. It has happened frequently in the past, and slackness has always meant casualties, lost rifles and little return in enemy dead. He will certainly begin early to trickle into dead ground as close as possible to the front line, to keep it on the jump and to be handy when the time comes. So keep your eyes skinned and watch. Groups in dead ground may well be missed by the planes, which ought to be freely used on these occasions, but lucky ground observation and a message to the guns may discourage them badly.

You will have thrown up cover, if in the front line for obvious reasons, if in support or reserve still throw it up, for it may be badly needed when the withdrawal begins and the withdrawing front line passes through yours. Your cover will not be a continuous parapet like that of the piquet rapidly growing behind you, but improvement of existing cover. And while on this, both on this work and elsewhere, you will find that men if not watched or until they have had their lesson, are apt to put up the "sangar" (lit. stone wall) of manœuvres, a sort of little card house of thin slabs of slate, much worse than useless. One of the reasons why the covering troops were pushed off the Black Hill at Palosina on December 23rd, 1919, was the stupid sangaring. All along their position were found these idiotic little cairns, so small wonder they were blown off by fire almost at once. And you will find that at first the men do not grasp the need for haste in improving their cover. Twice I found one of my battalions doing its best to lose ground it had taken without much opposition, the men loafing round and carrying up pebbles instead of rocks. And because its officers seemed to see no crime in it, it went on to communications defence. But do not imitate them in risking the safety of the entire force by such action.

The day passes, with occasional sniping shots wheeping over, and enemy pressure gradually increasing. Wounded and dead must be cleared off at once. I once watched an Indian doctor hold up a withdrawal by half an hour. He got a wounded man away, nestled into a cleft, dressed the wound, and then, a curl of smoke and great activity round a fire. One of my look-out officers told me what was happening, and a swift messenger was sent to haul the good Samaritan out. The poor little fellow, his mind full of Mesopotamian Commissions and what not, had felt it his duty to prepare a nice cup of Oxo for the patient before resuming the descent. Just shows what you have to look out for. Get wounded, dead, sun cases, everything that is going to hamper you, cleared out as they happen—there will be more than enough work for the stretcher-bearers at the end. Have your plan cut and dried, and communicated to all concerned, including those in support of you, and you have done all you can. The rest depends on the staunchness of your supports and the surefootedness of your men. And, a great deal, on luck, for an unlucky casualty at the very end may upset your plans badly.

In one way you are fortunate, if your battalion commander is wise. For here, if you go out from camp and return there, much of what a man carries on a march can be left behind. The towel, spare socks, waterproof sheet, toothbrush, emergency ration, etc., etc., can all be left behind, men clad as lightly as may be and carrying only a little food, water and ammunition. Lightly weighted men have a far better chance in work which, though on a larger scale, is carried through on exactly the same lines as a withdrawal from a piquet.

At last you are warned that the withdrawal is to begin. If you are lucky. Many a piquet covering party has been driven in before the piquet was finished, and then not only was the work to do again, but the immense advantage of fire from the established piquet was absent. So, for your own sake as well as for the object of the operation, hold on however hard the enemy press. Counter-attack may be needed to restore bits of your line—costly, yes—but you are killing tribesmen and at the last you know that an undisturbed supporting line is ready to cover you off.

If you have been able to dribble part of your men away beforehand, so much the better—otherwise at the arranged time or signal you clear, down into the quiet of some depression between you and the support whose bullets are now swishing overhead, through or around them and into the dead ground up which you and the piquet workers toiled in the early dawn. And so, halting to cover your comrades off, to the valley and to camp, a good day's work done.

* * * *

Under cover of that work another junior officer has been hard at it—the piquet builder. He left camp immediately behind the covering troops, with a party which, if experience has counted for anything, should be fully organized in every particular. It has to be, for the absence of any one thing must hold up the whole work. Of first importance is the party of sappers, with stakes and wire, whose particular task is to cover the front and flanks at least of the piquet with a well-established apron of wire. For though the small party it is possible to leave in one of these piquets may be overwhelmed, all that is possible to prevent this must be done. Not only to save men, or to economize in them, but to boost the *moral* of the garrison, and to assure them that if they are knocked out it can only be at a loss to the enemy which will make them careful how they tackle another such problem. Wire, then, is the first essential, and wire has to be aproned on well driven stakes, and stakes cannot be well driven on a bullet-swept hillside, so the sappers accompany the infantry party to work early, and quickly, and independently at the job. Stakes, coils of barbed wire, concertinas of it, jumping irons—you can leave the kit to the sappers. Possibly there will be some pioneers—lucky for you if there are—trained workers and stout fighters, who will bring the expert touch to the wall work. But your own men have to work, and work well, if the piquet is to be safe by night. You should dispose of, at the least, sandbags, shovels, picks (the last in good measure if you are to prize up rocks), a jumping bar or two, and men trained in peace to wall-building and hard, quick labour. Behind all comes a separate party, the piquet garrison with all their requirements, which they dump below the site and fall to work with the rest while the mules feed and stay handy till progress makes certain that they will not be wanted to take all the stuff back again. It may be preferable to let the piquet garrison come up later—in this case the mules are sent down as soon as off-loaded.

The requirements are many. Personal baggage, for the piquet garrison is to stay there some days, and must have comfort and warmth; ammunition reserves, lots of spare sandbags, grenades, Very pistol and lights, a coil or two of barbed wire, some spare stakes, a pick and shovel, rabbit wire if the enemy has had a chance of acquiring grenades, food for several days, water and means of storing it (the "diggi" again), cooking utensils, a lamp or two, spare dressings, some latrine pans and tins and disinfectants for them, and if the column has tents, the tentage allotment for the garrison to keep off sun and rain—a lot of stuff, but all necessary.

By the time it is light enough to see a few yards it should be possible to see enough to site the work, as its general siting will have been settled already, if only by distant reconnaissance. The sooner this is done the better, lest bullets interfere. The sappers spring to their job, completing the stake work before the wire goes on, and meanwhile the whole strength of the other workers fans out on the slopes nearest the enemy, and passes up all available stones to the wall builders, whose first aim is to raise a well-based wall to front and flanks. This done, all come round to the protected side and continue, several men filling and carrying up sandbags into the piquet as fast as possible while building progresses. Sandbags may be invaluable from the start if the enemy starts sniping on the builders, and in any case, the wall should be finished off with them to avoid bullet splashes, while of course they are best for loopholes and head cover. The wall slowly mounts, with a traverse inside if needed; the sappers finish the apron and wreath wire round, then complete the circle; the walls are topped with sandbags, loopholes are prepared, firesteps from which to meet close assault are started, spare stones heaped up inside and at the back, spare sandbags filled and stacked inside, and as soon as the cover is high enough for determined men to hang on to, kit is brought into the piquet, and the garrison takes post.

As soon as there is nothing for any party to do they should clear off—the Sappers when their work is done, the Pioneers as soon as the stone-walling is finished, the mules as soon as it is seen that the piquet can be ready, and the balance of the infantry as soon as the kit is stored. The garrison has already been told off to its alarm posts, ranges have been taken, sentries posted, and the walls manned. Long before this it should have been possible to pass word to the covering troops of the time they will be free to withdraw. Any refinements of defence work must be left till the covering troops have withdrawn and the enemy cease from troubling; as long as the work is complete enough for defence you have no right to keep the covering troops out, for each minute as the day grows late adds to their losses and difficulties and to the forces they are up against.

You may be sure they will withdraw as soon as they know you are ready; and now comes a very important part of the day's work. Be prepared to open fire, heavy and effective, on any point the pursuing enemy is likely to appear on, and have your walls fully manned, with several men using glasses, alert to spot an enemy. The more effective your fire now, the less chance of your being worried after the other troops go, and the greater the help you give the men who have been sticking a trying day so that you could get on with your work in safety.

The covering troops go, passing you in successive lines; the enemy will probably clear off after the first few rushes, except for a few snipers, and you are left to yourself and the night. Now for a sharp look-out, no exposure, and busy completion and improvement of the defences. Particularly the head cover. Without it you are always liable to have your men's heads kept down by accurate fire from a few hundred yards off, while others of the enemy creep up and attack by fire and by direct assault under its cover. The wire and grenades will save you a lot in such a case, but should the wire be penetrated and the walls reached, you must use the firesteps and shoot down the attackers at close range. Not till really close, when their covering fire must cease, and then you will find that though the tribesman is good in a rush, he is by no means so formidable when it comes to killing at point blank range. I know of only one instance when a walled piquet held by determined men has been rushed, and that was due to defective head cover. The Mandanna piquet was rushed in 1919, but the " determined men " condition was absent once its officer was killed. The stand of the unprotected piquet at Barwand in June, '17, shows what is possible to men who are prepared to fight it out.

* * * *

You organize your command in the usual way—a third on inlying piquet, the rest to work or rest; all sleep by the walls, and you yourself lie close to the foot of a sentry on the most exposed side. Reserve ammunition handy, filled sandbags also, and water well protected. Signal communication established with camp or with the large intermediate piquet we used to call the " mother " piquet, a covered loophole being prepared for emergency, and touch established with other piquets to right and left and across the valley.

Avoid panicky firing during the night. An electric torch is useful to investigate the wire apron from time to time, without the disturbing effect on other piquets of the Very Light; and if you can shoot a tiger by the light of an electric torch, you can surely drop a man.

The wire, by the way, can't be so far out as to keep the enemy outside bombing distance—the weight alone of a circle of wire of twenty-five yards radius would be prohibitive. But it will guard against men pulling down the wall by stealth, and against close assault. A rabbit wire pent roof will have to suffice against the bomber.

In the morning, stand to arms before dawn and again before anyone issues from the piquet. This, of course, must happen, for you can't be beleaguered all the time. Also, day latrines are needed—usually wise to have a little " sangar " built, and use latrine pans. A well-run system of permanent piquets will budget for visits on convoy days by a sweeper and clearing of latrines, just as it will budget for periodical visits to replenish water and food, and ammunition when needed. At these times letters, luxuries, and anything else you need can arrive, along with your company commander, who from his lair in the " mother " piquet issues to see that his various piquets are happy and properly run, and that nothing remains to be done for defence.

These visits must be made on convoy days, when convoy escorts help to strengthen the line; and on those days, if quiet reigns, your garrison can go off in driblets down to the stream or spring to wash and generally to relax, while those left in the piquet remain alert, questing the hills not only to their own front and flanks, but wherever an enemy can threaten any part of the line.

Your piquet may find it desirable or even necessary to watch ground at some distance. A day piquet must then be used. When it goes out, remember to take all precautions or the tale of the Tochi piquet may be and probably will be repeated.

Cooking, sun bathing, delousing, anything which can be done close to the piquet should be done under the rear wall, and small wing walls protecting the men so engaged are needed. For days may pass without any trouble and then one day some devil who is out for mischief may loose off at your kitchen, a well defined and accurately ranged target, and one or more of your men go west, a loss you could have avoided by a little work.

A senior officer, if he is experienced, will form his opinion of a unit by its performance of detached duties rather than by its appearance on ceremonial parade; and the routine of permanent piquets shows up a bad battalion quicker than anything else I know. I used always to look for the outer signs of a good piquet. Alert sentries, a clean, well-levelled floor, equipment neatly bestowed on pegs driven into the stones, ammunition and rations carefully stacked, water tank standing clear of the floor, and no dripping to make puddles and attract flies, bedding out to air, cooking place brushed, refuse burnt or burning, wire apron clear of papers, oiled rags, and all the debris which accompanies military life, some occupation for the men, a useful logbook for the piquet, a cleared space for aircraft message strips, and—the sign of the keen unit—some little bit of swank in the way of pebble-outlined pattern, regimental crest, or the like. But these I know we will be sure to find in your piquet. When I was young an eminent soldier said that for conscientious performance of unsupervised duty the British subaltern stood alone in the world. He was right then, and I believe I am right in repeating it now.

And it is all necessary, for a stretch of several days on end in the cramped quarters of a piquet would be deadly dull, if not bad for health, without interest in life and in care of men; go slack in this and be sure you and your men will grow slack in other things, and then Brother Pathan comes into his own.

That is what the system of permanent piquets implies—sharp fighting, heavy work, and days of dull but important watching by dozens of little detachments along a line of communications. But it saves Heaven knows what labour. And time. Convoys can start up the line from any post at any time after daylight, and return any time before dark, without the delay which putting up daily piquets means. A few intermediate and small daily piquets amplifying the control of the permanent ones will suffice, instead of the weary and often costly posting of daily piquets all along the line.; and convoy escorts, instead of being strong and then always on the jump, can be reasonably small, and move without anxiety. So initial losses and daily isolation are well repaid, and I think you will find that the permanent system on the line of communications has come to stay in any but the smallest or shortest of operations. I have told you what I can about them; and while I am on it, I may as well deal shortly with another frequent activity, escort duty.

Here, as I have just said, your work has been much simplified by the framework of permanent piquets, and you have only to do in a very small way what the advanced guard to a force on the march has to. The little van guard clears the way for the transport, for there may be a few men lying up who haven't been spotted by the piquets. Keep an eye open for the routine signal from a piquet, which means " Danger in the Offing," usually the displaying of a coloured flag, to attract the attention of all, and not only of signallers watching for a message. And as the van guard moves along, the troops behind it send up little groups to occupy possible lying-up places, small knolls or nullah openings to the left and right out of the reach of the van guard.

In all this, never relax precautions. The most difficult thing in the world to do is to force care on men who know that no enemy has been seen for days—but you must do it. A careless advance to a crest, possibly a careless supporting party, unready to open fire, and you have taken it in the neck once more. The enemy, knowing that in spite of the Manual's warning you must follow practically the same track day after day and occupy the same ground, has had ample time to watch your method and to work out his plan. And unless

H

you are ready for him he will carry it out and risk bolting through the permanent piquets by the dead ground, which of necessity exists in places, and you will go back cursing the enemy's "cunning," when, after all, the fault is yours for giving him the opportunity.

The convoy moves on dropping people who have all to be picked up later—a sanitary squad sent to disembowel and burn animals, casualties from the last convoy; a cable-repairing party; officers inspecting tracks; doctors carrying out inspection of piquets; and so on—and at last meets the down convoy—a stray officer or two and leave parties, sick and wounded, possibly some prisoners (a sullen lot these, and you had better remove their pyjama strings if they are truculent—it cramps their style), but mainly camels without loads, the last marked by a large flag. It passes the last of the up convoy, you exchange a last word with the van guard of the other escort, and turn about. Baggage escorts take up their place by the returning animals, and the whole move as fast as may be to camp and rest. You are now the rear guard, and the work of rear guard and piquets with a column is reproduced in miniature, but with equal care. The temporary piquets come tumbling down from their places, anyone seen in the valley is taken along with the convoy or sent scurrying up to the permanent piquets as the case may be, an occasional long range shot whines over the strings of camels, and the valleys sink back to quiet. Boring, perhaps, and trying, yes, but it is all part of war in the mountains, and you have to prepare for it or you won't be able to do it as well as you will be expected to.

* * * *

There is only one class of terrain where the permanent piquet cannot be fully useful and where convoy work becomes in consequence far more dangerous, and that is in the intersected and bush-covered " Raghzas " or plains fringing the foothills of most mountain areas.

Here command is absent, and therefore the permanent piquet, or indeed any form of piquet, loses most of its value. For the enemy can creep up unseen by any of the many ravines and attack through the scrub with everything on his side. He can only be met by movement, and this is just what is denied to convoy escorts, which will always be in danger in this type of ground.

The only remedy I can suggest is to clear the vicinity of the track to some two or three hundred yards distance on both sides, dragging the bushes away to form a knee-high entanglement until such time as it is needed for firewood. And in lieu of permanent piquets build a sort of stone pulpit every half mile or so, with a good high firestep and open towards the road, in a bastion of the entanglement, for occupation by little detachments from the daily convoy escort. These give command, and unless the enemy reverse the breastworks they cannot fire from them, and if they do, it can be spotted at once. While these are being made armoured cars are the solution, with command and protection, combined with a fire power and speed which gives them surprise properties of the greatest value. If there had been armoured cars to intervene at the Spinchilla fight in the Tochi, where these conditions obtained, a nasty minor disaster would without doubt have been turned into a crushing knock for the tribesmen.

* * * *

There is another possible activity connected with defence of the communications, which is very much a junior officer's job. This is what, earlier in this book, I called a "Floating Platoon." Properly handled, it should be possible for such a party to get much of the advantage of surprise otherwise mainly enjoyed by the enemy. There is nothing the tribesman hates like people getting behind him, and it should be, not easy, but quite possible for a handy and lightly equipped body of men to do it, with their front and rear and one flank covered by the permanent piquets and thus moving with considerable freedom about the hills under their support. Only, there must be no slackness in actual movement, and the variation of time and direction of march day by day, on which the Manual insists, can only be got if the party beds down in a different place every day. It may also move in the dark to known points of vantage on the chance of finding at dawn gangs which have also trusted to the dark to get unseen to the point they have selected for ambush. Such a move must be made early, soon after midnight, and must be a short one, for as I have already told you, patrolling in the dark is no use unless it is stationary. This sounds Irish, but has truth in it.

The main point to remember in your arrangements for your men is that no one, except the men in charge of your ration and baggage mules, yourself, and your second in command, should know till you have left your night's halt where you hope to fetch up that evening—for a bird of the air may tell the matter. And in your day tactics, alert scouting, constant sweeping with glasses and by the eyes of trained observers of the ground to be crossed, and on top of all, movement covered by readiness to fire, both of near-by piquets and of parts of your own command.

CHAPTER X.

ASPECTS OF WORK FALLING TO JUNIOR OFFICERS WHEN A COLUMN MOVES.

Early preparations and start of advanced guard—Preliminary work of rear guard—Duties with transport—Rearguard activities.

Now let us see what happens if the force is moving on. In all probability the route has been protected by permanent piquets for some distance ahead, and the camp site itself is similarly covered. In this case the object of the day's move will probably be to carry the column forward, perhaps putting up on the way two or three more permanent piquets in continuation of those established already, forge ahead a few—generally very few—miles, camp, and complete the grip on the communications by working back from camp. On the other hand it may be that the opposition does not justify this slow process, and that the order of the day is to be what, after weeks of steam-roller advance, the troops in 1920 delightedly hailed as " pukka Motan," or " Real Mountain"—the arrangements as practised of old. In such a case, the intricate work of piquet posting begins as soon as the advanced guard has left the circle of camp piquets, and the camp piquets themselves have to be withdrawn at the end. So we will take this case, as holding more to talk about.

* * * *

All have been warned, and there has been a buzz of preparation since an early hour. Inlying piquets have been alert from the moment of the " rouse," to cover the falling in of the advanced guard and of those accompanying them. The dawn patrol is not needed in the sector through which the column is to advance, but no other precaution can be missed. Up in the piquets kit is got ready, and at the first streak of light, mules or carrying parties move up and lift the stuff down to camp to be loaded and take up or catch up its proper place in the transport column.

The rear guard commander may have told the piquets overnight his plans for withdrawing them. If not, he sends word now, for on the proper order of their withdrawal depends a good start for his trying day.

The troops of the main body, if this heads the transport, may be moving shortly after dawn, for the advanced guard, which went out in the dark within the ring of camp piquets, has by now started a bunch of the flank piquets up the hills to points which its commander has settled on by distant reconnaissance the evening before, if he is wise and has had the time.

* * * *

Transport officers of units have drawn the first line mules. These have been made over to battalion headquarters and to companies, and those moving with the troops are starting. The rest, if they have not already fed, do so now. There will be no time to water them even if the animals will drink at this early hour, and they will either be in camp soon after noon or will have prolonged checks and opportunity to drink on the march. But they must not be loaded a minute earlier than is necessary for them to move to the exit and take their place in the mule transport which heads the transport column. So it is the duty of the officers left behind with the baggage guards, composed of cooks and employed men as far as possible, and of the transport officer, to see that loading is done quickly when it begins, and that the baggage guards, whether they are to march with first line or train, work full blast from the start, at whatever loading is to be done. Meanwhile the train transport, usually camel, is feeding, resting, and if there is time, watering. Their attendants groom and otherwise care for the beasts, and themselves get a good meal, for it is unlikely that the bulk of the camels will be leaving till well on in the morning, which means that they will not get to camp till late; and it is senseless for units to take them over and waste the idle hours before the start, when by using these the men and animals can start happy on the day's work, which no one knows the end of.

Why all this trouble about a lot of animals, I have been asked. And indeed, in my early days it was seldom the poor beasts or their attendants got any consideration at all. Most of the transport then used was raised for the campaign; raw and unfit animals scraped up, and a mass of untrained and unwilling transport drivers collected from anywhere. Some never met their animals till arrival at detraining stations or later, and most of them funked and loathed the mules and camels they had to care for. The officers were usually collected from non-mobilized units, and though they worked themselves to death, could do little, even with the help of a couple of sergeants almost as new to the game as themselves. The cooking and clothing arrangements were bad, no food was carried for the camels, and little enough for the mules, result— casualties among the men and animals, inefficiency, indiscipline, and waste. The wonder is that we got on at all, but in those days both enemy resistance and transport needs were less. Nowadays, anything like the same proportion of casualties among animals would lead rapidly to the disappearance of the camel, the most useful of our military beasts of burden, and already becoming almost a zoo rarity in India, what with canal irrigation, increasing cultivation, and development of motor transport. And then where would we be? So we will be wise to be more careful of him than of our men, who can be replaced; and if it came to a question of sparing the camel or sparing his attendants, baggage guards, and so on, I know which would go to the wall if I had the ordering of it.

You will find that a well-run column with a transport

head who knows his job will never allow animals to be drawn before they must be to get into their place in time, and you will find that pressure from above compels unit commanders to aim at never keeping animals under load before the time to start. This means rapid work by baggage guards and by the escorts of ammunition and supply columns, but it pays every time. So you, as transport officer, do not draw the transport earlier than you must, and then load it swiftly to get to the starting point at the time when your calculations, checked by the actual passage of other units' animals, show you that they will be needed there. A little delay is of no consequence, for however good the roadway, you can be certain of one thing—that the transport will soon check, and you can catch up.

Compare a transport column run on these lines, and the start from Shinawari in 1897, where, owing to the check at Dargai, camels were under load for twenty hours and more. Simply due to unintelligent staff work and units' desire to get an unpleasant fatigue over early and off to war. But the poor brutes of camels! Remember that while a man can sit down or lie down to ease his task, the camel seldom and the mule never can lie down under load; and be merciful to your best friends.

A lot of talk about the transport animals, but not a word too much.

* * * *

All this while sanitary detachments, working at half strength because half have gone on with the camp colour parties, are clearing up the site, filling in latrines and piling litter. No burning can be done because of smoke, till the enemy have ceased from troubling.

The baggage from piquets has reached units, loaded up, and gone on to catch up unit transport if too late to start with it. You yourself as transport officer have gone off with the last of your unit baggage unless called for other transport work; and the camp has slowly cleared, leaving nothing there now but the rear guard, possibly a couple of companies, some machine guns, and a section of guns either in position near the camp or a mile or so up the road.

If the war spirit is strong, the rear guard will have a hot time from the start. If very strong, and heavy rear guard fighting is felt to be likely, the column commander and the bulk of the fighting troops will move behind the transport ready to intervene or relieve the original rear guard. But this is unusual, except when the whole force is withdrawing, when it will be normal. Until the enemy is broken he will always oppose an advance into his country, and a show of strength in front will draw off opposition from behind, whether it be a fighting column or a line of communications or a piquet party taking up its position.

But if the country is nominally quiet, the rear guard still has an unpleasant task from the very start, and that is keeping tribesmen off the camping ground. They come along, unarmed to all appearance, and scavenge round for empty bottles, discarded grain, and so on. You cannot shoot if there has been peace and they obviously do not mean war, but unless kept at a distance by small piquets and loud threats they produce much confusion and may be dangerous if others less trusting choose to harry the rear guard at the same time. Besides, there is always the chance of treacherous attack. So the rear guard, bullets or not, has an anxious time from the start.

* * * *

As soon as the transport has got fairly away, the rear-guard commander begins his real job. If he has been able to make up his plan and tell the piquets the night before or before starting so much the better, and better still for all concerned if he has been able to relieve the mixed lot of camp piquets at dawn and let them go on to their units. However, the piquets, whether his own men or the old piquets, are called down in succession according to the tactical situation, each in turn following the same protective routine as we have seen followed when drawing down to the line of march. And thus the rearguard carries on, sending away surplus troops as they come down, first from the camp piquets and then from those sent up by the advanced guard, and generally doing its utmost, by co-ordination of the work of piquets and rear guard, to withdraw without the serious checks which will follow a lapse by either.

I should like you, if you ever have the opportunity and the inclination, to read the account of the evacuation of Camp Karamna in the Bazar Valley by the First Brigade of the Tirah Expeditionary Force, on December 29th, 1897, which you will find in " Frontier and Overseas Expeditions," a Government of India publication.

This, and the map accompanying it, will give you a far better idea of the ideal evacuation of a camp by a rear guard than anything I can say. It was a perfect example of how it should be done in face of considerable enemy activity, and holds lessons for all, junior and senior.

If you can do as well in your own part of the work, you are an expert.

CHAPTER XI.

ASPECTS OF WORK FALLING TO JUNIOR OFFICERS IN ATTACK AND WITHDRAWAL.

Opportunity for a " formal " attack seldom offers ; and must be taken fully when given—Distribution ; and points to guard against—Further action in case of an advance—Or of a withdrawal—Ravines and other dangers—Danger of intersected and bushy country—Night work.

A LOT has been said about various activities, but except where it was inherent in these, we have said nothing about the attack. This is not so remiss as it seems, for the formal attack is probably the least frequent of all events in this form of war. The first advance may have to overcome a stand-up resistance and there may be two or three such stands during the campaign, though, of course, the very infrequency of these makes it the more necessary to take full advantage of them. The trouble is, it is so hard to inflict real loss in an attack unless an enveloping move can be brought off, and even this must be limited in its effect.

For these people are firm believers in living to fight another day, however often it may mean bolting like rabbits; and it is quite impossible to " pin them to their ground." They have no communications to defend starkly, and their line of retreat is about as traceable as a markhor's. So, though the pursuit is always a very desirable thing, it is difficult to carry out except by gun-fire or by planes, and the scattered enemy gives few good targets for these. It follows that every use must be made of the few chances of inflicting loss during the advance, and many of these will be given only to the junior officer, so that a lot depends on him.

* * * *

An enemy may be attacked when found in position by a force on the march, but this is infrequent, for when a force is on the march the enemy prefers harassing from a safe distance and taking the chances which in-fighting with the rear guard and piquets offers him.

Usually, he will stand on some well-marked feature covering an important part of his country or, more likely, some part to which he attaches sentimental importance—some part which has never had its " purdah " lifted, as at Landakai the " purdah " of Upper Swat, the Tanga Pass into Buner, or the successive Dargai, Sampagha, and Arhanga ridges covering Orakzai holdings and Bagh. In such cases the force can move conveniently close and, with special precautions against night assault meanwhile, prepare to deliver an attack in form. The column commander need not worry much about major tactics—all he has to do is to select his point of attack and this enemy will conform. He did so at Chaharasiah, at Kandahar, and in all the lesser fights for positions of which frontier history is full. But a commander, in the plains at least, can often lay successful traps. Shabkadr in '97 was one example, where the tribesmen were drawn out into ground suited to cavalry. The Burjina Pass, April, 1908, was another, where the cavalry concealed the movement of guns into close range. I managed to work the same thing in a small way beyond the Khurd Khaibar in May, 1919. As I have said before, the " cunning " tribesman is very easily had.

* * * *

But we are getting away from the junior officer's job. First in importance is the distribution of your command. It will generally have to be in considerable depth, for the slopes up which you have to advance will not allow deployment to any extent. And other folk's commands will be using the spurs to right and left, so you cannot spread that way even if it did not mean that your command got out of your hands. If you can deploy two sections you will be lucky, but it does not matter really, for not only do you then have plenty of strength in depth in case you have to repel an attack, but, as it is next to impossible to inflict loss on men behind cover with direct rifle fire, your front of fire does not matter. What does, is the power given to a handy formation in depth, of pouring in a heavy oblique fire on an enemy opposing your comrades on other spurs, and hidden from them. Such targets will be more exposed to you, and deeper, and so oblique fire is far more damaging than an occasional casualty from frontal fire. Even these targets do not present themselves till you are nearing the enemy's cover, and your fire is then from a very effective range, so do not waste fire in the advance till you can use it really effectively. The guns, and to a lesser extent the machine guns, will keep the enemy's fire down, and machine guns and your own fire can deal with them should they expose themselves.

Your distribution in depth has another advantage. You are strong to resist assault, and this may come. If it does, look out for it coming from men lying up a little distance in front of the main position. These will be men who have accepted the fact that they will not return and who deliberately lie up in front with a view only to effecting a desperate surprise dash so that their try for Paradise may have a better chance of taking some of the attackers with it. The first time I saw this happen was at Landakai, where six Bunerwals, ages from sixteen to sixty, suddenly leapt out as the front line was closing and fixing bayonets for the final assault on the enemy's sangars. They came out from a fold in the ground, a mere furrow of rock some twenty yards below the crest, and went slap through three of our lines before the fourth bayoneted them. Armed only with knives and axes, too, stout fellows.

In the advance you move forward covered, if necessary, by artillery and machine-gun fire, without closing up, but waiting before the final advance to the assault till someone fairly close behind is in position to support the moving lines with close-range fire. This you must have, for if a charge comes in from anywhere, it comes in like rolling rocks, and unless someone is ready to open on it, the charge will get home unbroken. And, though your distribution in depth can deal with it, it can only do so after a most unpleasant bit of in-fighting.

To meet such attack, and because of the shape of the ground and the comparative lack of volume in the enemy's fire, your successive lines should be well closed up towards the end. Your advance is, of course, preceded by ground scouts in groups, never singly, until the enemy's position is neared, when the scouts halt and are taken on by the advancing lines. This, of course, to avoid loss from surprise attack and also because it is not sound to give the enemy the idea that you are getting close until you are close up in force.

One thing I want to warn you against. I have often seen the Lewis gun detachment take the gun and ammunition off the mules, toting the whole up hill, with Mr. Mule halting perhaps a mile from any danger. Do not do this. It is always possible to get the mule well up with little exposure, and I hold that the gun mule is a soldier and has to take a soldier's chance like his comrades the men behind the gun. But to do this you have to train both mules and men to moving on shaly and pebbly hill-sides. Otherwise the mule will slip and perhaps upset, and the man is even more likely to do so and haul the mule over with him. You have only to see a mountain battery from some plains station its first time on the stony slopes of, say, the Tochi, to see at once what I mean. After practice there is no reason why a mule with the easy load of a Lewis gun should not go anywhere a man can climb without using his hands to steady him. This was the old rule with the mountain guns, and a good one.

Another hint—do not halt your men on tracks or near conspicuous rocks, and so forth. These are always known ranging marks. And your men will not halt near you. " Officers and white stones "—the old soldier's rule still holds.

This is not a thing to neglect. The accuracy of these

people's shooting is sometimes astounding. I have mentioned the case of the Ahnai Tangi, when I was warning you not to bunch your men on a crest. This was not an isolated fluke. At Makin I saw four men knocked out by one sniper, known to have been fifteen hundred yards off; and shortly before that, taking up camp at Marobi, one man, who was bagged before he could do more damage, got two men and two mules in five shots, at a range of not less than five hundred yards.

* * * *

For several years there was a tendency to try to lessen losses by what some termed " prophylactic fire," consisting of bursts of fire loosed off at any point where the enemy was suspected to be. It meant a ghastly waste of ammunition and on more than one occasion I know that it led to the 150 rounds carried on the man being exhausted almost before the troops had closed with the enemy. In the attack it can be very useful if the enemy is known to be there, but otherwise it should be most sparingly used. In the withdrawal, when one main object is to avoid casualties and their hampering effect, it can be more freely used, and should be whenever there is reason to suspect that danger threatens from any place within effective range. Machine guns, of course, are the weapons *par excellence* for this.

Casualties in the attack must be cleared off as they occur. You never know when it may become impossible to deal with them. On easy ground stretchers may be used and give the wounded more chance. But on rough ground, where stretchers cannot be used, or when carriers are hard to spare, some method of carrying the wounded pick-a-back must be used. The puttee method is taught in India, a puttee being used to keep the man in position while his bearer is jolting and slipping down hill. It is the best way so far known and saves men, requiring only one carrier and another man to carry rifle and equipment of the casualty and of the carrier.

It has been found that the whistle is unsound. It gives away the whereabouts of the advancing lines to an enemy always a little shy of awaiting attack, and it also gives it away to anyone lying up to charge who does not want to betray himself by peering over cover. Signals combined with low-voiced words of command should be used.

The pace must be steady. For heaven's sake do not be led by false notions of regimental prestige to hurry faster than you can move without distress. If you read Hutchinson's account of the action at the Arhanga Pass, in the Tirah show of 1897, you will find an example of the gymkhana event which I want you to avoid—two battalions " having a great race up the hillsides," in " admirable rivalry." Think what would have been the result if a hundred swordsmen had come out on what could have been little better than a breathless and disorganized mob. If any further warning is needed—officers are more lightly equipped than men, and if you dash ahead you may be first up, but you may well be first off with a Pathan knife in your ribs.

Keep your men well in hand, go as quickly as may be consistent with arriving at the top in good trim, fix bayonets and close whenever the crest or a likely lying-up place is neared, and, arrived at the crest, pursue the enemy with fire at once and as long as any are within effective range. Hustle with fire orders. I am a heretic, I know, but I have seldom seen fire orders terse enough to take up pursuit of this enemy or to deal with his sudden attack. Enemy fire or assault, if not dealt with in some speedy way, may prevent the perfect fire order from achieving the result it is expected to, and I prefer to see fire opened, the emergency being dealt with, and then errors corrected and the men got into hand as quickly as may be.

* * * *

Further action depends, of course, on the commander's plan. He may be content with giving the enemy a knock; more likely he will have in his mind a limited advance to some suitable spot beyond. This will be the usual thing and the advance will continue. It is the commander's business to see there is no delay in pushing on—if there is he and you will pay. He, in mental strain while his transport is struggling into camp in the dark; you, in hunger and possibly stiff fighting in protection of the animals. But the junior officer can help in several ways. He can take steps to push the enemy back if not already in full flight; he can make dispositions for a fresh flying start; and he can save his commander much worry and his men much discomfort if he insists on their having, and carrying, solid food for the night and next morning, apart from the emergency ration. This seems superfluous advice, but it is a phenomenon of every campaign in which the British soldier takes part that he will throw away his food rather than carry it, trusting to a grouse to get more when as a rule there is none to be had. Nothing leads to full hospitals more quickly than empty bellies; and a commander's plans may be very much hampered if he knows that his men cannot be called on for an effort just because his orders have been neglected.

But let us suppose that the commander intends a return to camp after the fight. If the enemy have taken a good knock, the return will probably be quiet, but I should take all precautions and I advise you to. The commander has two great responsibilities. The first is to make his decision to withdraw as early as he can. Anything may hold the move up, and in the short days of winter in which a campaign usually begins, the day is short enough. It was delay in this which brought about the nasty incidents of the Saran Sar withdrawal in Bagh in 1897, and it was the memory of that which made me move back when the entrance to the Ahnai Tangi was almost in my grip on January 7th, 1920.

The second is to direct the main lines of the withdrawal and not leave the troops to find their own way. Again, the Saran Sar.

The rest falls on the air force and the troops, and especially on the junior officers, though the unit commanders have a lot to think of.

The moment you learn the orders, fill up pouches if not already done, and send all animals back except those needed for actual fighting loads. Then dispose for covering fire in the withdrawal, if this has not been provided for by other troops, and if the enemy is close push him back. At the least bomb him or direct fire on him. I have never used smoke grenades or other means of laying a smoke screen in action, but I imagine that now they would find their real rôle. For the tribesman will not waste his precious cartridges on a target he cannot draw a bead on, and smoke to screen a sudden attack or in a withdrawal to cover the flanks against enemy fire may be really useful.

Thereafter, withdraw on the lines I have already wearied you with. Train your men to move fast and to glance behind them from time to time, for now is the time this training is going to be useful. The Manual gives you one good reason—to see if a comrade has been hit—but there is another one, to see if the enemy swordsmen are not rushing along behind. I have watched, and sickened to see, a couple of men struggling clumsily down a steep ravine into the Takki Zam, separated from their comrades and others, and behind them two Mahsuds bounding in pursuit from rock to rock, nothing in their hands but knives. The first those two men knew of their nearness was the knife-thrust. Less than a mile off, and powerless to help, it was a ghastly thing to see, and yet if those men had been decently trained the Mahsuds were easy money.

* * * *

The withdrawal should be easy with proper dispositions, but there is one thing to look out for. At the foot of all slopes you will find nullahs. Water-worn ravines, small to begin with and tempting cover, later becoming deeper and narrow, impossible to keep men closed up in, and hideously dangerous. Unless both sides are held as the Manual says, avoid them; and remember, if they have to be entered, do not trust to other dispositions to make you safe. Ravines wind in the most astounding way, and the protection of other troops may disappear at any moment with a turn of the nullah, so you must supplement their help with men of your own up in the open.

The Manual, in fact, sounds a little casual in its warning, " Ravines should be avoided," etc., because it was written for use by men with some experience of India, where the ravine warning will be rubbed into you soon enough. In spite of this, it is astounding how often the warning is ignored. And how often trouble follows. The reason no doubt is because of the feeling of safety which the deep ditch of the ordinary nullah gives, and it is only human nature to seek cover from storm or danger. The trouble is that in a nullah you cannot see if danger is coming near, exits up the sides are usually few and bad, and the farther down the nullah you go, the steeper cut and higher the sides. And when an enemy, however few, spots a party in such a position, you can be sure that it will be rounded up and shot down with a minimum of trouble to the enemy and a minimum of chances for the sinners. And the shots being drowned between the cliffs, with little chance of assistance being attracted. So follow the book closely, and, in addition, if there is any other way out available, side-step the nullah or you may find yourself in the position of the Northamptons' party coming back from the Saran Sar in '97, where they lost some good men, the enemy got some good rifles, and one of the best friends of my youth went west.

And, remember, in this connection, when advancing to attack watch carefully for any such difficult place which you may have to deal with when withdrawing, and be forewarned.

At the foot of these hills you will often find flat

ground cut up by nullahs and covered with scrub jungle or grass clumps. Then fix bayonets and watch out. I have already warned you about this—" the bush-covered and stony plains and ravines where the dashing tactics of the Mahsud find their fullest scope." Here is where Mountain Warfare fails as a title, for this sort of ground cannot be described even as hilly, yet it is by far the most dangerous if cleverly used by the tribesman. In mountains it is always possible to get command, whether one has to fight for it or not. Here there may be none, just a network of ravines, bewildering to the foreigner, but well-known ground to the tribesman, and when you add low clumps of bush, all grazed down and consequently dense, for him to approach behind and take cover behind, you will see that it is possible to meet much nastier propositions in the plains than you do in the hills. The mess-up at Manjhi in October, 1919, was one, and we found more when preparing for the advance to Palosina later in the year. Two bitter little scraps and a lot of sniping cost us eighty casualties in three days, with little to show for it. Later, a most dashing attack on a strongly guarded convoy in the Tochi, near the Spinchilla Pass, showed that the Mahsud had remembered and that we had neglected the danger of such ground.

Armoured cars are invaluable here, if they can move, having command, protection, fire power, and speed, but without these aids an attack on troops in this sort of country can only be dealt with by movement—counter-attack or steady withdrawal, with such arrangements for covering fire as can be made. They will be few enough, but as long as the troops are not stationary the enemy must move, to escape or to follow up, and then only will they give targets. Incidentally, command without protection is little use. At this Spinchilla affair, part of the escort, very naturally, rushed and seized a little bare rocky knoll, from which they were picked off by men in the bushes, without hope of retaliation.

I suppose I ought to say something about night work, as this will often form the first part of a move to attack, whether on an enemy in position or to secure a desired point.

In the old days our armament was much superior, an advantage which darkness neutralized, and several other factors operated to make night work a thing to avoid. We gave up, for instance, all the advantages of discipline and fire power to take on men in their own ground and well accustomed to night movement on it, and so it was seldom done. Climo's relief of the hard-pressed camp piquet at Kharappa in 1908 was a notable instance, the more so as such a thing had never been heard of before. But in 1920 the short hours of daylight made it obligatory to lengthen the working day, and the enemy's accurate rifle fire made it desirable to blanket its effect by moving in darkness. Several moves of large and small forces were begun in darkness with great success, which again was partly due to the cold, which induced the Mahsud, always an individualist, to prefer the warmth of his huts and caves to watching for his cause all night in the wind and wet. And when he took it on he could not resist wrapping his head up. We nearly got some on their cots in front of the Barari Tangi, and later, in the Tangi itself, a party was surprised and dealt with faithfully. But I am far from saying that night work should be undertaken lightly, and would only try it if a big advantage offered or necessity compelled me.

If you have to take part, you can best prepare by training your men in peace to move in the dark quietly and sure-footedly and to use collected fire when ordered, or the bayonet in silence, if they are lucky. Reconnaissance is never possible except from a distance, and here sensible use of glasses and previous practice in the study of hilly ground will never be wasted. These can, I find, be best used in memorizing land-marks for use as distance checks on your road. Compass bearings are, of course, necessary, but as your route has to be a well-defined one, you will find that there is generally something, a stream-bed, a nullah mouth, a tree trunk, or a bit of cultivation, which will guide you better, the compass bearing being a check and a comfort.

Air photographs may be most useful, allowing not only study of routes for the approach march, but of probable posting of troops on arrival at the objective; and your commander will be well advised to use them freely in deciding on your moves, more especially when these are lengthy or have to be carried through out of sight of any ground within our occupation.

And if your move is successful, it is a great thing to feel you have bamboozled the enemy, saved your men loss and your commander time, with possibly a bit of damage done to the enemy, either on the road or as he bolts under fire from lairs you have passed.

* * * *

There is one thing I forgot. It seems obvious, and it is often forgotten. When advancing to the attack, or when withdrawing, or indeed at any time, never set light to anything as you pass unless ordered. A " bhusa " stack will put up a dense smoke and in a moment all chance of visual signalling is gone. You will often find that a light-hearted man or, and more often, an unsupervised follower, puts a light to something, a hut or straw shelter, out of pure devilment, and the damage and delay throughout the day will soon show you the need for care yourself and for a sharp look-out for possible sinners.

CHAPTER XII.

Aspects of Work Falling to Junior Officers in Foraging and Demolition.

Foraging equipment—Organization for the work—Points to be watched, and methods found safest and best—Constant vigilance needed—Method of withdrawal—Demolition, a more serious matter—Organization for the work, and methods of destruction—Manner of withdrawal.

WE have dealt with marches, camping, permanent piquets, convoy work, attack and withdrawal. What other activities are left? Two, certainly, in which the junior officer has a lot on his shoulders. Foraging and demolition.

In these, as much as in any, organization and fighting qualities are essential. Organization, for time, always the essence of success, here becomes its quintessence; and fighting qualities, because the work is always carried out by comparatively small forces.

Take foraging first. This is usually done when the area searched is fairly quiet, and in day trips. Unless it can be done thus, the supplies gathered are not worth the labour of gathering and bringing back, for they are mostly bulky things, and hard to carry and load, and the stuff all needs cleaning before use. But it may be necessary for moral effect or because supplies are not coming up the line.

The first thing to see to is that the men have means of cutting and that the transport destined to carry the stuff back take suitable means of loading. Sickles, for instance, for the standing corn. A battalion has none and the Gurkhas, quite rightly, will not lend their kukries, so the Staff will have to arrange for sickles or something of the sort if they want green fodder and effective foraging. Nets are needed if mule loads are to weigh more than a few pounds, whether green corn or bhusa. Sacks will be needed for grain, but all sacks and packing material are handed in as emptied to the Supply people, so these will have to be drawn. Then some Pushtu-speaking men should be detailed to go with you; and while all these things are outside your power to procure unaided and should be arranged for you by those ordering the foraging, you should see that they are available before you start.

The troops should be organized into several lots, with any of which you may be. Troops to cover the move to the area selected, which piquet the route and throw out piquets covering the work from a distance. Troops which on arrival post protective parties covering the work from near by. Troops for the working parties; special troops to move back early with live-stock, which moves slowly; troops to assist the transport personnel to tie up and load; a reserve, not to be used in any work, for you never know what may happen; and a rear guard, which becomes the advanced guard for the return journey. Foresight and organization are required for all this, which usually falls to a senior officer to see to. But you on your side can ensure that your men are trained to work all out, and that they do so now. And that they carry food for the day and for the night.

In the outer system of defence your work is no different from what we have already gone through, with the same precautions in taking up positions, in holding them throughout the day, and in the withdrawal. On the inner line you have only to keep moving to see that your men are fully alert and not interesting themselves in the collection. Your least difficult though most tiring work will come if you are in charge of the working parties. Here you have several things to look to. First, do not let your men work individually—each group must be under control, each with their own definite task in their own limited area. They all work accoutred, arms slung or close to their hands, because in this work men must move about and cannot pile and unpile arms every moment. They must work concentrated because the work is done as quickly and more safely, and each party must work with at least one man ready and on the alert, guarding them closely against assault. It was at Nahakki, I think, in the Mohmand show of 1908, where three greybeards, ripe for Paradise, dashed from hiding on a few pioneers and took five with them as a passport.

Drive your men all the time. Taking other folk's property is so new an activity that they will waste time at it if you do not check them. No ragging, no chasing after hens, no looking for souvenirs. Particularly drop on taking Korans out of house or mosque. They are holy books and family bibles; they are no good to the despoiler and taking them is a dirty trick. Set light to nothing and watch followers, who need it. And stop looting—by which I mean taking stuff for personal use. When all is said and done, looting is only a euphemism for stealing, and if that does not make you pause, it also means waste of time and leads to indiscipline, so stop it dead.

Any villagers found in the place or its vicinity must be taken to the village meeting-place and kept there under guard till someone in authority interrogates them and either decides to treat them rough or deals with their requests. You often find old, blind, or otherwise useless mouths abandoned in the houses. I need not tell you to be kind to these, and the troops generally have to be restrained from looking after these helpless folk.

* * * *

One area cleared of whatever you were set to collect, move to another, piling stuff as gathered in some handy central place for the rope and net parties to deal with. But do not straggle, or you may suffer as did the foraging parties in Maidan in 1897, November 6th, I think. There the entire foraging force split up smaller and smaller till the Afridis, who were prepared to be good as long as it paid them, found the chances too good to be missed, and there was a nasty mix-up, which would have been much worse if it had not been *impromptu* on the Afridi side.

* * * *

Even if friendly arrangements have been made for the late enemy to furnish supplies, no precautions can be omitted. He may have the supplies ready; if so, the work of the foraging parties is less and all can concentrate on the roping up and loading. But do not be friendly, even if he has souvenirs for sale. Let those whose business it is to talk to him do so, and you and your men mind your own business, and not the least important part of that is to be alert. For the tribesman with a melon in his hand can change into a danger by dropping the melon and pulling a rifle or sword out of the roof, and if you are slack you may be tempting the poor devil beyond bearing.

Be particularly alert in the rear guard work on the return journey. For the friendly tribesman, having collected payment, is by no means above chivvying the rear guard home. He can always blame the bad men from the next valley (who may be—probably will be—there also on their own), and the rear guard, though it may have an easy time, ought to behave as if it expected trouble. If it does not, the odds are on getting it. And that is another reason against delay in any part of the work. Every moment wasted means a closer approach of evening and of increasing numbers of the enemy intent on harrying the withdrawal.

The day wears on. The morning's rear guard moves off, live-stock close behind. Mules are called up and loaded, and move off at once with their baggage guards, the late roping parties. The workers assemble, close in their protective groups, give the animals a fair start, and move off as main body, staying in rear where most likely to be needed. The outer line of piquets is then called in, the order of their withdrawal carefully thought out by the commander and every precaution employed in the actual withdrawal of each. A rear guard grows out of the piquets, which move along withdrawing those along the route in the usual way. On arrival in camp, loads are taken to the appointed place, ropes, loading nets, sickles, sacks, etc., are handed in, and a discharge for them taken, and so to a well-earned meal.

* * * *

That is easy enough. A far bigger proposition arises with demolition. For here you are not collecting supplies from a comparatively quiet locality. You are going out to set your mark on a stubborn enemy, to punish him for years of accumulated evil-doing in the only way bar killing that has the least effect on him. There is usually an outcry about this form of punishment, with good reason. I dislike it intensely, but after the enemy's will to stand and take punishment is broken, there is no other way to make him watch his step in the future, or if there is we have not found it out in the past eighty years.

And it is a big proposition because, unless the enemy is completely crushed, he will rally to defend his property or revenge its loss, and you will find him fully as fierce as a wasp in a harried hive. During the destruction of Makin in 1920 this was very marked. Makin was an Abdullai holding, and, though there could not have been more than four or five hundred of them in the field, on the first day the price was thirty-four killed and twenty-eight wounded, and on the second day twenty-seven killed and sixty-three wounded. On the third day the sting had gone out of them. We had only twelve casualties that day and twenty in the last two days, for it took five working days to lay Makin out thoroughly. Fifty-one towers and over four hundred and fifty main dwellings in various hamlets in the cultivated area were destroyed, and most of the retaining walls in the fields, figures which show how slow such work must be when opposed. Here I would say that it is far better not to attempt destruction unless it can be vindictively thorough. To singe and run away is costly in proportion, has no lasting effect, and the enemy is no end cheered at the lightness of his punishment, and soon forgets it.

* * * *

If a large area has to be dealt with, the commander of the force will be well advised to move close up to it, enclose the part with piquets, and employ his whole force in covering the work and in destruction. In Makin we could only deal with parts of the area at a time, with bitter fighting; but we were dealing with the Abdullai, stark fighters with a good grasp of collective work, and we had to put out our full strength to make good the area we were going to destroy. Guns in action at three hundred yards' range on one occasion, and so on. If it is a lesser locality it may be possible to move there, destroy, and return in the day, or to occupy villages for one or more nights and make a job of it. In any case, it is unsound to take on more than can be carried through thoroughly—we do not want a repetition of the opening days in the Mamund country in '97, where the force split into three and tried to do in a day what should have been a four days' affair; with the result, of course, that all three portions were badly hustled, and the job was left undone.

But whatever the plan, organization for it follows the lines of foraging. That is—a force sufficient to secure and cover the work, groups providing inner protection, and strong working parties preparing for demolition. The protective arrangements must be thorough, though it will seldom be possible to ensure the workers being fully protected from fire. It must suffice if the enemy cannot attack without losing heavily, and that, of course, is better than all the houses down.

With the troops told off for the duty, there will be,

or should be, sappers to do the more difficult demolitions, and guns for their ordinary work and also to deal with towers and so on which are strongly held, and in some cases which are in localities too difficult to get to without undue loss of time and life. Tools for infantry should include picks, billhooks, crowbars, rope, saws, oil, portfires and matches. Parties are told off to such jobs as can be foreseen, and a reserve of working strength kept handy. The sappers should blow down all towers as quickly as possible. After a little practice they can gauge to a nicety the charge required, and make the tower collapse as gracefully as a lady curtseying, which is the thing to aim at, as then the infantry need only be taken off work from quite near the explosion. The infantry start preparing the houses on a broad front, and with the mud houses of the frontier this is a pretty strenuous job. Some like blowing out the corners and lighting the debris. A quicker way is a big draught hole dug in the roof, furniture and firing material heaped on the floor, and oil or ghi thrown on. The great thing is to produce flame enough to burn the cross-beams if not to ashes at least so much as to render them useless for roofing purposes, and to weaken the walls so that they must crack and crumble outwards under the thrust of a new roof. The walls have then to be rebuilt and new roof trees cut, brought from far off, and seasoned, all requiring time during which the victims can brood on their sins.

Any helpless inhabitants must be removed to some suitable detached huts, and you will find the soldiery doing their best to get the local kittens and puppies away. Grain, if not taken away, should be heaved into water or, failing water, heaped in the open with a good lacing of oil poured on the cone, and left to be lit at the end.

There will be plenty of work in the houses, fairly safe from snipers' attentions. More dangerous and equally necessary work is in the open, where parties should be set to work pulling out key-stones in the retaining walls which hold up the terraced fields. The Gurkhas are particularly good at finding these, for their own fields are built up in the same way. But the knack is soon learnt—a few heaves with a pick, out comes the stone and several feet of the wall comes down with a roar, with earth following. Then before that part of the field can be any further good, the earth backing has to be lifted and the wall rebuilt—a year's cropping lost, during which year the sinners pay for their sins.

Another job, still more exposed, but very effective, is finding the water channels and destroying them; look for a point where it runs along a cliff and blast or pick out several feet. The repair generally calls for experts and these often have to be imported, so the labour on this is well spent.

I do not like ringing trees—it seems a crime against Nature; but it may have to be done, or the trees done in with guncotton, if large, as were once the holly oaks of Marobi.

But all these things require time, so the more saved by previous organization and by steady driving, the more successful the result will be.

Now we are up against a problem—smoke. The houses have to be burnt and that means smoke, and smoke means loss of visual communication, and that means difficulty in drawing off the protective piquets of the outer line, or the troops in positions covering the work, whichever method is adopted. It follows that the covering troops must know, and as early as possible, what the procedure of withdrawal is to be, and that an unmistakable and simple signal for commencement of withdrawal must be fixed.

Take it that the houses are all ready for lighting. The parties in the fields are warned to come in, portfires are lighted, and on a signal, say, a Very light followed by another at an interval of half a minute, the portfires begin their work, systematically firing the houses at many points, but beginning on the leeward side lest any worker be trapped in the narrow alleys. Each house should be fired and all oil-soaked piles of grain, but if time or the enemy presses, light only the houses on the windward side and clear. By the way, look out for bees. A certain Highland battalion might still tell you, if decency permitted, of the value the men got from their kilts in saving their faces at the expense of other parts when the bees of Maizar resented the burning of their homes. Another argument, if one were needed, against indiscriminate burning of houses.

* * * *

The two Very lights can well be used by the covering troops as a signal to take preliminary steps for withdrawal, and as soon as the officer in command of the operation sees that his working parties are clear he should send up, say, a red Very light or even a star shell as a signal for the withdrawal to commence according to plan. The working parties and the reserve will have taken up positions to help their protectors as soon as these pass through the screen of smoke, the flanking parties are withdrawn in due course, and the whole force combining fire and movement, as usual, to safeguard the withdrawal and inflict losses where possible, returns to camp or, if out for the night, to a hitherto untouched or, if prepared, unlighted village for the night.

Hot, dusty, dangerous work, but frequent, and therefore you should be prepared for it, by sound training in the principles and method of advance and withdrawal and by constant thought over the most time-saving methods of organizing for work.

TO SUM UP.

THAT is all of use I can tell you. But I think I have said enough to show that, as the Manual says, while the principles of war remain unchanged, " The tactics and characteristics of the inhabitants and the nature of the theatre of operations may necessitate considerable modification in the method " of their application to warfare on the North-West Frontier of India. And that unless a good working knowledge of the methods indicated by experience is learnt in peace and applied in war, trouble if not disaster is bound to be the outcome.

But I also hope I have made it clear that previous training, energetic and common-sense application, and unrelaxing care will give you and your men complete ascendancy over an enemy whose great natural advantages at first sight may seem to be unchallengeable. And I trust what I have been able to pass on of my own experience and of my observation of others will help you in this.

If so, I have discharged my debt to those who taught me and to those who taught them, and to those, my comrades in war, with whom I proved the truth of those teachings.

INDEX

	PAGE
Advanced guard commander at work	25, 44-45
,, ,, ,, duties of	42, 62
,, ,, duties on march	24, 31-32
,, ,, ,, on reaching camp	25, 62-63
Aeroplanes, air photos	118
,, co-operation in fight	29, 89, 114
,, reconnaissance needs confirmation	21
Ahnai Tangi, enemy marksmanship	47, 111
,, ,, Flathead Piquet contested	76
,, ,, Vanguard ambushed	32
Alarm posts	54, 77, 78, 80, 83
Alarm, action in perimeter camp	82
Alertness constantly needed	6, 32, 96, 97, 122
Ambush, enemy, well equipped for	7
,, examples of enemy, and our own	7, 8, 32, 108
,, in rear guard action	56, 60
Animals, care of	102-104
,, in night attack	82
,, in withdrawal	54, 114
Arhanga Pass, undue pace in advance	112
Armament, tribal improvement traced	13, 14
Armoured cars	20, 99, 116
Artillery " screen "	46
Assault on attacking troops	109
Attack, covering fire in final stage	109
,, distribution in	105-110
,, enemy, rapidity of	46, 110
,, Ghazi, dangers of	83, 85, 121
,, oblique fire in	109
,, on camp, action during	82
,, ,, always possible	64
,, ,, reserve's duty	73, 83
,, on transport, work of guards	38
,, pace uphill	112
Baggage guards, distribution and duties	27, 35-36, 102, 104
Barari Tangi, enemy misled	10
,, ,, night surprise	117
Barwand Piquet's stout stand	76-94
Battalion equipment animals	33
,, transport	33
,, ,, personnel, duties	34, 36, 102
Bayonets, when and why fixed	47, 50, 82, 112, 116
Bivouac shelters pitched parallel to perimeter	78
Black Hill, bad sangaring	89
Booby traps, suggestions for	9-10
Bunching punished	47-48
Burjina Pass, example of ruse	108
Burning, smoke of, stops signals	118, 126
,, start systematically	126
Bushes, best cleared near defences and track	74, 77, 99
Bush forms, learn names of	66

129

K

INDEX

	PAGE
Cable cutting, suggested deterrent	9
Camels, difficulties with	36
,, reasons for sparing	17, 103
Camp colour parties	26, 65-66
,, defence (*see* Perimeter Camp)	
,, defences, types	66
,, duties (Chapters VII and VIII)	63-85
,, laying out	65-68
,, natives barred from	84
,, piquets (*see* Piquets, camp)	
,, reserve	72, 83
,, routine in	83, 84
,, work on arrival in	65, 73, 77-78
Careless battalion asks for punishment	8, 43
Casualties, clear early	52, 89, 111
Close assault on piquet, use firestep	94
Coats, warm	49
Column on the march	24-30
,, size of, cause of increase	15, 26
,, work on starting	101-106
Communications in camp	77
,, in defence of village	79
Company commander in piqueting duties	27, 28, 44, 53, 55, 95
Control of Frontier areas, ideal military evolution	18
Convoy escort duty	97-98
Counter-attack, to relieve pressure	60
,, to remove casualties	59, 60
Cover must be bullet-proof	89
Covering parties	48, 62, 74, 77
,, troops, work of, in piquet building	88-91
Crests, avoid exposure on	47
Cunning of tribesmen, and counter thereto	2, 4-11
Dakka, noisy piquet	75
Datta Khel, wild firing incident	80
Dawn patrols	83
Dead ground	20, 47, 54
Defence of perimeter camp	67-69, 77-78
,, of piquets	74, 75, 93, 94
,, of village	79
Demolition	123-127
,, covering the work	124
,, Makin as example of	123
,, organization for	125
,, steps described	105-126
Depth in attack	108
Detached bodies for flank protection	43
,, posts from piquets	48, 49, 95
Deterrent fire	111
" Diggi," a useful equipment	74, 78, 92
Distribution for demolition	124
,, for foraging	120
,, in attack	108-109
,, on perimeter	68
Dressing stations	68
Duties in a battalion	70

INDEX

	PAGE
Equipment, special, and foraging	119
" " for demolitions	125
" " for piquets	71, 92
" occasion for reducing	90
Escorting convoys	97, 99
Examples of defence of piquets	
" of neglect of principles	46, 50, 115
" of night assault	64
" of tribal cunning	4-7
Fields, destruction of	126
Fighting qualities of tribesmen	2-3
Fire, oblique, value of	109
Fires, dowsed in attack on camp	82
" precautions against	79
Firesteps in piquets	93, 94, 99
Firing at night, must be controlled	80
First Line Transport	33
Flank piquets (*see* Piquets, Flank)	
Flares	19, 68, 82
Flat Head piquet	76
Floating platoon	6, 99
Followers, position on march	27, 35
Food, must be on person	113, 120
Foraging	119, 123
" distribution for	120
" equipment	119
" organization	120
" precautions	120-121
" withdrawal from	122
Garrison of camp piquets	72
Ghazi attack	53, 83, 85, 109, 121, 122
Gibraltar piquet contested	76
Grain, destruction of	125
Grenades	19, 54, 73
Guard, personal, against treachery	53
Guides into camp	40, 66
Guns, action of	20, 24, 28, 43, 58, 88, 104
" improvements	19
Hairpin bends, and effect on camels	36
Head cover	74, 94
High velocity rifle main factor in changes	12
Historical review of changes in armament	13-14
Huts, grenades for clearing	20
" preparation for burning	125
Identification of strangers	85
Infantry in attack	108-111
" on perimeter	63
Inhabitants barred from camp	84
" in foraging and demolition	121, 125
Inlying piquets	78, 82, 101
Intelligence agents	85
Invisibility increasing	13, 14
Irrigation, destruction of	126

INDEX

	PAGE
Kapurthala piquet disaster	50
Karamna camp, good rear guard work	106
Kharappa piquet, its losses	46
Khurd Khaibar, ruse	108
Khuzma Nullah incident	7
Korans, respect while foraging	121
Landaki, attack on advancing infantry	109
Landmarks in night work	117
Latrines, bad dressing stations	68
,, night, sentry over	84
,, provide early	66
Laying out camp, unit's allotment	66
Leapfrogging	24, 28, 30
Lewis gun, in camp defence	68, 69
,, in support	45, 54, 59
L. of C. protection, by permanent piquets	16-17, 96
,, ,, convoy work	97-98
,, ,, in bush and scrub	99
Loads, first line, keep roped up	78, 84
Look behind you, reasons	57, 58, 114
Loopholes, low sited	73
,, signalling	73, 94
,, ware rifle snatching from	80
Looting	121
Lumsden's teaching not altered	23
,, training notes	41
Machine guns, advantage in armament	19
,, ,, covering movement	19, 25, 28, 43, 47
,, ,, in perimeter defence	68, 69
Mahsuds, fighting value	2
Maidan, foraging incident	121
Makin, deluding enemy	10
,, faulty air information	21
,, opposition to demolition	123
Malakand, attack on	64, 82
,, visibility of enemy at	13
Manjhi, disaster in broken ground	116
Manual of Operations, N.W.F. of India	16, 23, 24, 41, 42, 43, 44, 73, 97, 115, 116
Marches, length of	16
Methods on frontier little altered	23
Misleading enemy, examples	10, 11, 108
Mobility of tribesmen	2, 46, 109
Motorable roads, case for in future	15, 17
Movement of a column in mountains	24-31
Mule must be trained to hills	110
Nahakki, ghazis at work	121
,, scouts caught	46
Natives of country, keep out of camp	84
Nawagai, outlying piquets	69
Night assaults, action in case of	82
,, ,, always a possibility	64, 82

INDEX

	PAGE
Night movement, reconnaissance for	117
,, ,, value of air photographs for	118
,, noises, caution	74, 75
,, occupation of villages	79
,, work and preparation for	117-118
,, ,, recognition signals in	9
,, ,, reason for, in 1920	117
Nili Kach, vanguard ambushed	32
North West Frontier in brief	1
,, ,, ,, inhabitants	2
,, ,, ,, Manual of Operations	16, 23, 24, 41, 42, 43, 73, 97, 115
Nullahs and their dangers	115
Oblique fire, opportunities in attack	109
Observers, training essential	3
Outlying piquets are " wash out "	69
Outwitting the Pathan, examples	10, 108
Pace in withdrawal	57, 114
,, uphill, must be steady	112
Palosina and Umbeyla compared	13-14
,, scene of night assault	64
Patience of tribesmen, examples of	4-8
,, ,, how countered	8-10
Peace training in various activities needed	2, 3, 42, 57, 92
Perimeter camp, cover first need	69
,, ,, defence in	68-69, 77-80
,, ,, depth, how provided	67-68
,, ,, principles of lay-out	63
,, ,, reasons for	64
,, ,, routine in	83
,, ,, reserves in	67, 72, 83
Permanent piquets	16-18, 87-96
,, ,, action of troops covering building	88-91
,, ,, cover for men outside	95
,, ,, firesteps	93, 94
,, ,, garrison assist covering troops	93
,, ,, ,, signs of good	96
,, ,, head cover in	94
,, ,, mother piquet	94
,, ,, organization for building	91-92
,, ,, ,, for defence	94
,, ,, requirements in	92
,, ,, routine in	95
,, ,, sanitation	95
,, ,, signalling	94
,, ,, time needed to establish	87
,, ,, value	16, 97
" Permissive Signal "	55
Pioneers	25, 27, 91
Piquets, camp, advanced guard take up and help in erecting	62
,, ,, detailing, suggested method	71
,, ,, garrison	72
,, ,, infantry occupy, on own front	72
,, ,, must be held to the last	76

INDEX

			PAGE
Piquets, camp, reinforcement at night			... 71, 117
,, ,, relief of, when marching			105
,, ,, requirements in			71
,, ,, signalling			73
,, ,, Véry lights, use of, in			75
,, flank (Chapters V and VI)			... 41-61
,, ,, advance to			... 45-46
,, ,, " all clear " signal			... 29, 58
,, ,, bird's eye view of work			... 24-29
,, ,, casualties			... 52, 58
,, ,, company commander's duties		29, 44, 53-54
,, ,, counter-attack			59
,, ,, crest line, caution			47
,, ,, dead ground			... 48, 54
,, ,, detached posts from			48
,, ,, effectiveness of system			28
,, ,, Lumsden on			41
,, ,, must be held on to			50
,, ,, opposition to posting unusual			43
,, ,, piquet commander's duties with piquet		48-50, 54-58
,, ,, piquet slip			... 41, 44, 45, 52
,, ,, plan for withdrawal made known			... 48, 50
,, ,, rear guard commander recalls			56
,, ,, rear guard flag, when used and why			55
,, ,, reconnaissance of withdrawal			49
,, ,, road sentries			... 45, 48, 50-52
,, ,, screen			46, 57
,, ,, withdrawal			... 54-59
,, inlying			78, 82, 101
,, outlying			69
Pointer staff			... 44, 45
Precautions, never relax		6, 83, 86, 88, 97, 121, 122, 128
Prisoners			98
" Prophylactic " fire			111
Protective colouring of tribesmen			7
Punishment awaits slack unit		... 6, 43, 46, 47, 89, 97
Pursuit, great difficulty of			107
" Puttie " method of carrying wounded			111
" Raghza " dangers			99, 116
Rain and slipping hillsides cause alarm			75
Ranging marks, avoid			110
Ravine and scrub, dangers of			99, 116
Readiness to fire, interpretation			46
Rear guard			28, 29, 56, 59-61
Recognition signals for night work			9
Reconnaissances for various purposes		32, 34, 49, 115
Reserves in camp			67, 72, 82
Reverse fire, protection from			... 66, 68
Revolvers, precaution advised			84
Roads, case for, in future			... 15-17
Road sentries			... 45, 48, 50-52
Routine in camp			83
Ruses			8-11, 108
Sandbags in piquet building			... 71, 92
" Sangar " cover must be bullet-proof			89

INDEX

	PAGE
Sanitary detachment	66, 104
Sappers	25, 27, 32, 36, 91
,, usually in camp reserve	72
Saran Sar, trouble in nullahs	113, 115
Scouts, precautions in advance	46, 110
Scrub and ravine, dangers	99, 116
Shabkadr, scene of successful ruse	108
Shin Kamar, result of leaving piquet position	50
Signalling from piquets	73, 94
Signals, recognition for night work	9
,, Véry lights as	126
Size of columns, causes of increase	15, 26
Skyline, don't bunch on	47
Slackness risks early punishment	6, 43, 46, 47, 89, 97
Smoke equipment, its uses	20, 114
,, of burning, complicates withdrawal	118, 126
Snipers, controlled by flank piquets	28
,, firing at, to be checked	80
Spies	85
Spinchilla, armoured cars needed	116
,, example of scrub and ravine	99, 116
Spurs, use in advance	45, 108
Stalking at night unsound	9
Stampede, action of baggage guards	38
Star shell	19, 82, 127
Strangers, identification of	85
Supports to flank piquets	27, 53
Supporting lines	54, 58, 60, 90, 109
Tents, pitch parallel to perimeter	78
,, strike if enemy assaults	82
Tochi piquet, shows enemy's patience	4
,, floating platoon caught	6
Towers, destruction of	125
Training, special, in various work	3, 15, 42, 92, 120
Transport column, increase of	26
,, drawing and return of	34
,, importance of care for	101-104
,, must not be kept under load	104
,, must not park on march	38
,, officer, duties	33-40, 102
,, organization for frontier war	33-34
,, routine for, when force moves	102-103
,, staling halt	39
Treachery always possible	53, 85, 105, 122
Trees in demolition	126
Trench mortar	20
Tribal armament, improvement traced	13-14
Tribesmen, their cunning	2
,, their fighting qualities	2, 3
Umbeyla situation reproduced at Palosina	14
Vanguard, action of	24, 31-33
,, ambushed, examples of	32
,, opposed seldom	32
,, reports, road work needed	33

	PAGE
Véry light as a signal	126
,, ,, a valuable new aid	19
Villagers, treatment of	85, 121, 125
Villages, demolition of	123-127
,, occupation for night	79
Visual training	2
Wall, retaining, destruction of	126
,, village, preparation of	80
Wana, night assault penetrates	64, 83
Water channels, useful punitive demolition	126
,, party	26
,, reserve in piquets	74, 92
Whistle, use sparingly	112
Wire for protection	69, 71, 91, 94
Withdrawal after various activities	29, 54-59, 90, 113-116, 122, 127
,, ambuscades during	60
,, position of main body	105
Wounded	52, 58, 60, 89, 111